SILENCED BY SOUND

the Music Meritocracy Myth

Ian Brennan

Foreword by Tunde Adebimpe

Photos by Marilena Delli

Silenced by Sound: The Music Meritocracy Myth
Ian Brennan
© 2019
This edition © 2019 PM Press.

ISBN: 978-1-62963-703-7
Library of Congress Control Number: 2019933009

Cover by John Yates / www.stealworks.com
Photos by Marilena Delli

10 9 8 7 6 5 4 3 2 1

PM Press
PO Box 23912
Oakland, CA 94623
www.pmpress.org

Printed in the USA.

(This book is designed to potentially be read randomly, opened to any page and sampled. The content here is intended more to raise questions and stimulate reflection than provide any definitive answers.)

for
Noce
&
Noce di Cocco
(whose curls were born first)

Oblivion Embrace

Memory is nonlinear. Those experiences which are strongest seem closer in time or even ongoing, while the majority simply fade.

A person much wiser than I once told me, "Everyone thinks their own family is more interesting than it actually is."

I offer details of my own life not because I hold the slightest delusion that anyone cares about me. I do so only in the interest of specificity—the attempt to make words flesh.

The personal recollections contained herein are never meant to sound self-pitying. It didn't require traveling to Africa to understand how ridiculous and unjust has been my degree of good fortune.

Most of all, however clumsily, I was loved. And for that alone I am blessed beyond all measure.

Rather than "Who knows what evil lurks in the hearts of men?" we can just as easily flip that phrase to "Who really can fully fathom what goodness lies hidden inside another?"

CONTENTS

II. FALSE FRIENDS:
The Perils of Underestimation

III. MUSIC MATTERS:
The Trivial Should Not Be Trivialized

V. RAISING OUR VOICES:
Singing Back the Tidal Wave

VI. LOSING THE HUMAN RACE:
Compartmentalization Coffins

VIII. FAMILY RESEMBLANCE:
We're All Just Passing Through

AFTERWORD

PREFACE

Silenced by Sound is a companion and follow-up to my fourth book, *How Music Dies (or Lives): Field Recording and the Battle for Democracy in the Arts*. Streamlined and incorporating more narrative pieces, *Silenced by Sound* approaches the broad subject of inequity in media distribution from a somewhat different and more personal angle.

But the overarching message remains the same: *popular culture is far from the triviality it is routinely treated as*. Instead, it has far-reaching effects—going so far as to infiltrate people's homes and stalk their psyches through images and earworm hooks, ones that people often can't rid themselves of even when they desperately try to do so.

Justice at most levels of society is something that the average person can have little influence upon, and this leaves the majority of us feeling helpless, complacent, or impotent. Pop music, though, is a neglected arena where some change can concretely occur—by exercising active and thoughtful choices to reject the low-hanging, omnipresent corporate fruit, we can rebalance the world, one engaged, conscious, and committed listen at a time.

So many artists I know have confided that music saved their life. The music they created then went on to save others, as the many breathless backstage visits and fan letters attest.

Music is medicine. But people in the "First World" are overdosing on bad drugs. Worse, we peddle and pawn off our surplus to largely unsuspecting, less-advantaged regions. Still, at its deepest music heals, acting as trip wires for the soul.

Popular music, which arrived as a liberating force, sadly now more frequently confines.

FOREWORD

I'm sitting in front of my apartment building in Los Angeles, giving the immediate environment a listen. It's not a noisy street. Fortunately, the block is lined with trees that rustle in the breeze as cars and trucks roll by leisurely, the low whoosh of the tires and engines taking up the low-end space of things. There's a helicopter landing at a nearby children's hospital, and the midrange of its blades wafts up and fades, giving way to an open pocket where a few anxious sparrows can be heard chirping out a top line. A car alarm in the near distance and the wind chime in a neighbor's window jump in on occasion to add to the tune.

I am listening, and all the world's a song.

The question of what the song is about falls to the birds, as everything else making noise *has* to due to being mechanized, but the birds *want* to sing. What do they want? In most species, the males are doing the singing, and they do so from exposed perches to attract attention for their songs and for the song to be broadcast as far and wide as possible. They sing long and strong to let potential mates know where they are and to keep away potential challengers. The older birds are, the more songs they know. The amount of time a male spends singing clues in a potential mate to his endurance and experience, the ability to provide, survive, and give her the greatest chance of raising healthy chicks. In the courtship rituals of some birds, both genders engage in a complex duet that strengthens their pair bond and lets other single birds know that they are off limits. Bird calls are also used for different types of general communication, like letting a mate know about a new food source, calling a partner to incubation duty, or keeping birds in touch with one another while in flight. Ornithologists have observed that sometimes birds sing without any apparent territorial or court-ship concerns. On those occasions, the beauty of the song and joy of singing it might be the sole reason they vocalize.

The need for connection. The same reason humans make music. One bird could be Bo Diddley telling all those pretty women to stand in line, so he can make love to them in an hour's time because he's a bird, spelled B-I-R-D, and another could be Beastie Bird Mike D telling everyone that he's "created a sound that many were shocked at and has got a million ideas that he ain't even rocked yet." These other birds: Marvin Gaye and Tammi Terrell, or Kenny Rogers and Dolly Parton, going on about being islands in the stream, no one in between, no mountain high, no valley low, no river wide enough to keep them from each other. Last summer there was a weird bird who would pipe up regularly at about eleven every night and scream its head off to absolutely no one until roughly four in the morning. I looked it up and found out that this bird is a Northern Mockingbird, and honestly that bird could be me and almost every single one of my friends who make music—screaming in the dark, and maybe someone hears it, maybe not, but the point is: I can hear it, so I'm gonna do it until someone stops me, because nothing makes sense. And it's fun.

When I think about how music has shaped me, I have to project backwards to my conception. I was lucky enough to be born to Nigerian parents in St. Louis, Missouri, in the 1970s. That they were born in the mid-1940s meant that they were part the second generation in Nigeria to have access to radio or recorded music (with the Federal Radio Corporation of Nigeria having been founded in 1933 by the British colo-nial government), so they were awash in oral tradition *and* recorded music as part of the fabric of life throughout their childhoods. This meant hearing Yoruba songs of thanks and praise, cautionary folk songs, hymns pre- and post-Christianity's arrival, the muezzins' call to prayer across town, the vendors in the market singing to advertise goods, lullabies passed down through centuries, wars, famine, drought. By the time they were born, the British government's Radio Diffusion Service was up and running, allowing the public to hear the BBC's foreign radio service broadcasts in certain public locations over PA speakers. I'm guessing there was some classical music in those broad-casts, but one of the first search results for "British Music in the 1930s"

informs me that the influence of American Jazz had led to the creation of British dance bands, whose music began to dominate social
occasions and the radio airwaves. So into the fabric of Nigerian song
entered blasts of European classical music and a very tame, secondhand version of black American classical music.

By the time my parents were in their teens, the RDS had been reor-
ganized into the Nigerian Broadcasting Company and had broadcast
stations not only in the westernized capital city of Lagos—where my
mother's family lived—but regional subsidiaries in the relatively rural
cities like Ilorin, where my dad was from. For the first part of the day,
you could hear the local news in your native tongue, hear local musicians and bands—possibly on their way to national fame—and, and
later on, hear the news of the country, news of the world, and James
Brown. With the introduction of portable transistor radios in the 1960s
a million tiny speakers blew another layer of melody and fuzz into
the air. Almost everyone could get next to a radio, so they had a portal
to new sounds, new worlds. Somewhere in that era, at age fourteen,
my mother laughed off my dad, who tried to serenade her with a Nat
King Cole song at a high school dance in Ibadan. Yet, by some miracle,
fifteen years later I was born.

I remember my dad showing me how to record my voice on his
tape recorder when I was about five, and I spent hours talking, making
up stories and singing everything I could into it and being pretty
amused at how I sounded on tape.

My dad played piano and loved classical music and jazz. Brahms
and Beethoven sat in my parents' record and cassette collection along-
side King Sunny Ade and Chief Ebenezer Obey, Fela, Diana Ross, Ella
Fitzgerald, and the Beatles. Something was always playing.

We moved back to Nigeria in the early '80s and, like everyone I
knew, I was convinced that I was Michael Jackson, and that this (whatever "this" was ... life? third grade?) was indeed *Thriller*. I remember distorted, busted marketplace loudspeakers, playing prerecorded
vendor songs, and also actual vendors in the street, singing about their
wares, and Bollywood soundtracks coming from VHS/Beta tape kiosks.
Cassette releases from local and national highlife, juju, and religious
bands were available cheap at kiosks all over the place, and my brother
and I always walked away with one or two when we went out shopping with my mom. I remember listening to a bootleg tape of The Real

Roxanne and UTFO on my Walkman in my dad's home village at my grandfather's daylong funeral a few hours after a group of musicians had sung my father's family doxology. I had heard my name in the song and was later told that every Yoruba name and word could be played tonally on a talking drum.

I remember later figuring out that jamming paper into the top holes of any cassette tape meant you could use it to record the soundtrack from *Breakin'* and be the de facto leader of your fourth-grade breakdance crew, because you had the only dance tape and had salvaged the discarded cardboard box from a recent fridge delivery.

We returned to America in 1985, and it was exciting to read about rap starting in the Bronx and the roots of punk and New Wave on the Lower East Side and to then see the pattern over and over again: Make a new thing out of nothing. Not only *can* you, but you should. And if you want to hear or see it, you actually have to do it, because no one else can make your particular shape.

All of the music that makes me want to make music sounds true, and by that I mean that it sounds like someone is telling me their truth about who they are—where they've been, the times things went well for them, the times they didn't. A story, rooted in a personal truth.

Mainstream media will always seek out the authentic or "underground" and try to market it to people and "make it better." How do you sell black music to racists in the '50s? Elvis Presley. How do you sell Art Rock to sexist homophobes? Limp Bizkit. It's easy!

I remember a conference call with the head of our then label (a major we'd just signed to) after our album *Dear Science* did well in a bunch of year-end critics' lists. He congratulated us on "dominating" the charts, which we hadn't—reeeeally. And hearing a sixty-something-year-old man congratulate you on dominance feels exactly as gross as it sounds. He then asked us what the next step was and whether we wanted to take it to the "next level." A deep hush fell over the void at the center of the conference call. "The next level" in our case—given the label that we're talking about and how they judge success—was something to be approached with caution. The question was to be read: "How do you want to change what you're doing to sell millions of records? And don't worry, we are full of *incredible* soul-crushing, credibility-annihilating ideas if you don't have any."

New hairdos? Skinny jeans?

A hit-making star pop producer to work on the single?

Fergie?

Now that our band had some attention, the question was What level of lucrative lie do you want to tell to "ensure" commercial success? He asked us to think about it and let him know. We never got back to him. We just made another record.

I sometimes think of media today as a fine mist, with so much of it in the world. But then I think, it's always been this way. Technology has just upped the ante for short attention spans and distraction. The thinner mist of sounds that soundtracked my parents' teenage years got passed down, crept into my childhood, and then thickened over my adolescence. It is still present and growing deeper. And it is still helping me orient myself in the world.

The composer David Tudor talked about wanting sounds to be free, about the beauty of sounds appearing to be alive in a space, seeming to flow by themselves, unhindered by intention, intellectual or otherwise. He spoke about putting yourself in a situation of unpredictability, accepting it an observer, and realizing that sound can be free.

Ian Brennan has gone into many unpredictable situations, and he does what a great producer does. He listens for a long time, and when he hears the story, when he hears the song, he hits "record." And when the song is over, he hits "stop." Much like a nature photographer's job is to provide a clear portal to the thing that they're witnessing, and a meteorologist's job is to observe and relay the magnificent ways weather blows, Ian has a deep respect for nature, for music as nature, and he has dedicated his life to capturing, preserving, and sharing story and sound in their natural habitat.

I count myself very lucky to be a listener.

Tunde Adebimpe
TV on the Radio

INTRODUCTION

I try to never forget that there are more places around the world than not where I am the "wrong" color.

White supremacy, no matter how unintentional, positions whiteness as the norm. But statistically, it is the deviation.

As a teenager, I worked night shifts cleaning up human shit—a minimum-wage job for which numberless hospitals nonetheless refused me due to my long hesher hair, youth, and gender. When one convalescent facility finally dared to hire me for this oh-so-very-glamorous position, my first night's hazing was viewing the death of an elderly woman—a patient whose diaper I'd just changed hours before.

The rare times my family ever ate out, my mother would grab all the extras that she could get—emptying the takeaway condiments containers while we kept watch, shoving them into a purse already overstuffed with ketchup packets, paper napkins, and salt. It was a free-for-all, an attempt in one sweep to make up for all the times she'd been cheated.

Most anyone who is reasonably empathic gravitates towards wherever there is injustice. As an obese and cripplingly shy kid with a developmentally delayed sister and mentally ill mother, I felt little choice but to act protectively. Witnessing my sister's recurring social dejection, I grew up tensed and at the ready.

In San Francisco, a female jazz trumpeter once refused to play with me after she showed up at a gig and discovered that I wasn't black. For some reason, she'd mistaken my voice as African-American on the phone (an assumption that speaks volumes) because my register was "low." That she was a blonde WASP only made the irony all the richer.

9

None of this discounts my multipronged advantages, though.

I am painfully aware that on paper I am among the worst people to provide platforms to lesser-heard regions and populations—Caucasian, middle-class, straight, and male. By the same token, my wife, Marilena Delli—who does all of the photos and videos for these projects—may rival the best: raised in a factory (where her family squatted for an entire year without heat or electricity after the mill closed, the jobs having been outsourced to China), "mixed-race" from the most racist part of fascistic north Italy, and with a mom that survived two genocides in Rwanda that cumulatively claimed every one of her immediate family members.

But what works on paper often remains there—flat.

For any endeavor to take air and soar, it must actually be lived in real time. This is why supergroups that merge dream teams of stars almost always fail. What is too good to be true often is *too much* of a good thing—one ingredient canceling rather than enhancing another. Similarly, technology often fails at human scale since not everything is quantifiable, even that which remains unmistakable nonetheless.

Magic cannot be fully accounted for. It is the product of too many coinciding forces.

Synopsis of Critical Challenges

1. If you toss a dart at a map of the world, you are most likely to hit a country that is underrepresented or entirely unrepresented in international media.

   a) And if they are represented at all, it is often by stereotype.

2. Essentializing entire countries or habitats by spotlighting lone artists is almost more damaging than ignoring the regions altogether.

   a) Even most hardcore music lovers cannot name a single musical artist residing outside of those "foreign" countries that have been sanctioned as special and über-musical like Brazil, Cuba, and Mali.

   b) And even from these few (*relatively*) privileged nations, usually only a sole artist is known (e.g., Nusrat Fateh Ali Khan representing nearly two hundred million people in Pakistan; Nigeria, the most populous nation in Africa, telescoped to just Fela Kuti). This restrictiveness comes even from the rare people who "care" at all about international music in the first place and thus ostensibly should know better.

PROLOGUE
Don't Call Me Baby:
I wrote you a love song
on an air-sickness bag

It was at 3:13 a.m. when I realized that my fate wasn't to go deaf from the decades I'd played with loud rock bands, but instead due to a single screaming baby during the wee hours of morning.

And just as suddenly I feared that her first word would not be "Dada" or "Mama" but "Fuck!!!"

For months prior, my wife and I had been receiving the ultrasound readings as if transmissions from a space landing in peril on the moon.

Why do babies love white noise so much?

It must be the static sounds of the womb.

Every baby is born a prizefighter. Having survived their own arrival, they suffer PTSD from the delivery experience itself. And almost every child is conceived from parents that have made it to at least twelve years of age, so we are all forged from survival. More than evolution or progressing, mankind stumbles clumsily forward.

Even the most mundane moments fill my daughter with the wonder of a new universe. And that remains the challenge: to remain receptive, no matter how long any one of us endures.

Babies are better singers than we will ever be—little arias and operas punctuate their daily needs. It is only in order to conform to culture that they are forced to restrict their vocalization to pre-scribed sounds, with a resulting loss of musicality due to this sacrifice. Similarly, bilingual inflections—as lovely as they can be—are scars, consequences of all the sounds a person has been denied by their mother tongue.

Drunk with breast milk, babies find repetitive sounds tiresome and turn towards the novel, that perfect hit-song balance between variation and familiarity. And few things soothe a baby more than rhythm.

So it is that I became a human jukebox spouting made-up ditties.

Infants are among the most savage critics in the world—feet shot straight up in the air like an applause meter. Contrastingly, they cry and sigh, looking away bored—almost ashamed—for jams that just don't pass muster. They are microregional hits, known in my house alone.

Uncannily like some sort of sci-fi scene, I am forced via my daughter to travel backwards in time and care for a miniature me. Nonetheless, somewhat paradoxically, this act is best done selflessly.

It is unsettling to know that some of the deepest memories that I will ever form are experiences that my daughter is neurologically destined to have no recollection of.

When I hold her, I see a composite of almost everyone I've ever loved and those who've loved me, as well as those that have loved the people who loved me. Many of those, I did not ever even meet or do not remember having met. It is through this largely anonymous chain of equanimity that every new life manages to survive.

The only place you should want your baby born is in your arms. Instead, the rich today often curate hand-selected birthplaces, traveling across the Atlantic for the claim that their child was born in Florence. As the child earns no rights of citizenship for the wear and tear, the location is all superficial, only symbolic.

I harbor no secret ambitions for my child. Only for her to be herself, whoever that may be. A child shouldn't be held as captive audience to deposit the parent's unfulfilled ambitions. The only expectation I have is that she not deliberately harm anyone else, nor allow another to actively injure her. For to tolerate such an assault ultimately damages the assailant as well.

I know as soon as she can stand, she will start running ... away from me.

So I hold her while I can. And whisper private poems in her ear. Songs arise from her presence alone—out of shared minutes—melodies that live and die on the air surrounding us, never to be revisited.

My daughter is the dream I never knew I had.

I.

DE-RIGGING THE SYSTEM:

Spitting Out the Spoonfed Shit

1

Lopsided Representation: many "too manys"

The music industry has a dirty, dark secret. And it is the faulty concept that the entire enterprise is founded upon.

There are millions upon millions of talented people around the world. And you will never hear any of them. Many are as or far more gifted than the superstars that billions of dollars are depleted promoting the delusion that these lone wolfs have been blessed with genius far exceeding the common man, careers kept afloat by artificial life support.

But on a planet of seven billion people and counting, few things could be further from the truth. And so the gatekeepers make disappeared the platoons of to-be-forgotten or not-ever-known voices that singly could make some overhyped talent like Adele sound tinny and tone-deaf in comparison.

It is this lie that the media mafia are forced to maintain in order to continue the scam that they perpetually perpetrate upon the public: that beauty and inspiration are beyond the reach of everyday life, that magic resides outside of us, and can only be ours if bought—rented on loan.

The reality is that music is within us all. We carry it everywhere we go: stamped in our vocal cords, palms (snare drum), and heels (bass drum). Yet since the dawn of the pop era we've been hypnotized into believing that a choice few elite are so much more gifted than we mere minions, that we should do nothing other than fall dutifully silent. Their superhuman skill? Combining a handful of rudimentary chords, notes, and phrases into elemental structures. As a capper, we have to even pay for the privilege of being oh so fortunate enough to be allowed to listen.

Genius is a torch, not a state—an adverb more than an adjective. Springsteen is not a genius but is gifted and did genius things for an album or a few... at best. The brief flickerings where God murmured faintly in his ear.

If Bob Dylan stopped making records after *Blood on the Tracks*, the world would be no worse the wear. If U2's last album had been *Joshua Tree*, today there would be millions of dollars in reserve as a cultural trust. Instead, it was blown on half-baked inspiration and coasting. If Springsteen had ended with *Nebraska*, the world would have been saved the Rambo-rock caricature that followed. And that the Rolling Stones have not made a solid album since 1978 must mark the year that their storied pact with the Devil expired.

These are one-trick ponies whose shtick has worn thin.

Every new troubadour messiah should be reminded that they are not Bob Dylan. And even more importantly, neither is Bob Dylan.

Professional "personalities" pimp out their own persona, twisting themselves into affectations until they end up impersonating themselves, often illegibly. This creative devolution is marked by the passage from artist to entertainer, through which they become their own best cover band.

The telltale sign of a strong record is that one has such an excess of great songs that some can be jettisoned. Instead, the norm is artists grasping desperately for enough quality material to justify a foreordained release, even taking drastic and extravagant measures like recording in the Bahamas or the south of France to find their muse.

Pop culture is in dire need of a tough-love intervention.

Here is a basic rule of thumb ratio: the more money spent on a project, the more lacking its core. For if someone is burning to communicate something badly enough, it doesn't take them years and budgets of hundreds of thousands. Instead, they do it against all costs and obstacle.

Even more important than the majority of records that are not granted a fair shake of being heard are the millions of albums that simply never will get made at all—songs that are lost forever, dying with the physical death (or even earlier, through the spiritual surrender) of their creators.

2

The Myth of Heroic Authorship

In an era when citizens theoretically have the opportunity to listen to more voices than ever before, they are exposed to fewer.

As a direct result, the music industry is not dying as many people misconceive but is actually *growing*—generating revenue of over $50 billion a year.

Yes, we live in a world where Justin Bieber concerts gross $4 million a night.

Despite over one hundred thousand albums being released annually in the USA alone, the majority of countries will have no widely distributed releases internationally. But it is not for lack of product. It is based on the reality that most music remains imprisoned within its own linguistic borders.

And, this disproportion in distribution is not a case of the already preposterously unfair odds of 100,000 to 1, but 100,000 to *zero*.

Extrapolate that out over a decade and we have a million-to-one (or worse) odds, an indefensible and unsustainable equation for any semblance of democracy.

Meanwhile, as inventors of most one-way communication technologies, the English-speaking media has pervaded almost every corner of the globe for decades and recolonizes the world daily with Western imagery.

The songs linger long after the departed are gone.

English is the third most spoken, but debatably most hated language in the world. Many who speak English as a second (or third or more) language do not *choose* but are forced to speak it for their own economic survival (unlike someone learning, for example, Finnish or Cherokee purely out of admiration for the way they sound). One Portuguese musician I know goes so far as to refer to English as a "speech impediment."

Anyone who thinks that everyone in a given country speaks English just hasn't traveled deep enough in, far enough off the beaten path—even in Italy and France.

Unknowingly privileged people from the West often protest that it is "difficult" to listen to music in a foreign tongue. But this argument is highly selective. For if that same person was pressed to recite the lyrics to the majority of pop songs that they "know"—including those they have heard hundreds of times—they would prove completely unable, even in the case of their favorite songs.

If then asked, at minimum to provide a synopsis or gist of what a given song is about, many listeners would be unable to do even that. In fact, they instead often falsely believe that the song contains the exact opposite of its literal meaning.

"Born in the USA" is a patriotic jingle?

Hardly.

(Instead, it is the tale of a Vietnam veteran, traumatized irreparably.)

Unwittingly on point, a typical defense of vapid or offensive lyrics is, "I don't listen to the words anyway."

What avalanche of outrage would result if for even a single morning every television and radio station in New York City blared out nothing but Basque? Yet, this is the equivalent that has been and continues to be the case for almost every other place on the planet since at least WWII.

A solution?

I propose that artists past their prime be issued anti-recording contracts—paid to *stop* releasing music and thereby to help unclog the cultural circulation system of excess and refuse, halting the collective aesthetic bloodbath.

Even better would be retroactive recording contracts—whereby legends would receive just rewards for annulling and *un*releasing their more lackluster material.

Does the world really need another Neil Young song? Did he really have more than one (or *maybe* two) to begin with?

Do we really benefit any longer from hearing yet another group of white, straight males whine to standardly tuned guitars?

Not an iota as much as we'd profit from listening to an artist from the Central African Republic or Laos or *anywhere* but *"here."*

For the soy decaf café latte and coconut water budget alone of the latest corporately tied-in and timed single, hundreds of albums from the least wealthy nations could be made instead. But in their stead, we are offered up gilded turds, slathered as "comebacks"—the ever-reproposed return-to-form hype.

We are blue-balled ceaselessly by promo-machine-fed false prophets, spitting out confectionary misdirections. Anything to keep us from thinking beyond blinding, sponge-like whitened smiles.

Can you hum one song by Bon Jovi from the past three decades? Or Paul McCartney? Sting or Roger Waters?

Yet who here has not involuntarily been bombarded by "Living on a Prayer" at the mini-mall or "Comfortably Numb" while boarding an airplane or standing in line at the bank—held hostage and force-fed piped tuneage.

How many artists are there that you can get past your hands counting the number of irrefutably incredible songs harvested from throughout their generations-long career?

3

Freed Speech

In a truly democratic system, music would be released with complete anonymity: no photos, no names, only music.

Songs without faces and bios. Just sound standing on its own.

Historically, corporate controllers lost money on 80 percent of releases. Consolidation has made business far easier for them. They now profit off a spare few individuals, force-feeding those to the masses rather than experimenting and championing diverse sources.

It is the listeners who are the cheated by this manipulation and hoarding. It is we who've been victimized.

Looking for Love in All the Wrong Places

He believed that his arm was bionic, sporting nerves that had been replaced with wire cables by the government as he slept. He would flash his left hand in front of you as quickly as he could in an attempt to prove his strength and the speed of movement that he was convinced couldn't be detected by the naked eye.

He also wrote as tender and touching a ballad as I've ever heard.

The song was called "Water." It spoke of his desire to be washed clean of mental illness. And it is now lost forever. But its melody was so strong, I can recall the refrain, even though I heard it only once.

His name was Dennis—a street person, "rough sleeper," a Vietnam combat vet, and paranoid-schizophrenic—as if that were not already clear.

Those with schizophrenia usually possess greater awareness than we do, literally hearing things—real or imagined—that we don't, can't or won't. The illness is not so much due to a lack of awareness, but a surplus paired with the inability to filter and distinguish the environment's barrage.

Seeing a song so intricate dissipate is part of what sparked my quest to document the mightily worthy but little-heard.

What dreams must have lived inside his head as he floated past, almost transparent?

Healthy Disruption

You should not feel the same after a song is over as when it began. If it has not changed you in some way, it has failed.

Entertainment is amnesia. But art contains elements of suspense, making us look inward, to connect with ourselves and others more deeply, remembering the core of our humanity.

Art makes the world suddenly foreign and questionable, cracking our shell emotionally and rendering listeners smitten to a song.

Unless music evokes something in that you didn't know was there or fortifies what you aspire to, then people would be better served pulling out their earbuds and instead listening more closely to the sounds of their immediate surroundings.

I aim for a more immersive relationship to sound—much like how unstruck, sympathetic drone strings on many instruments are what carry texture to the listener. It is at the moment of decay is the point where instruments take on a life of their own, beyond the player's control—a beginning, not an ending.

If you are going to play conventional instruments, at least try to play them in unconventional ways. This mirrors neurosurgeons who force themselves to eat and write with their nondominant hand to develop ambidextrousness.

Breaking patterns is the universal aspect of all interventions throughout psychiatric history—no matter how misfired. And emotional health can largely be measured by the ability to embrace change and adapt, letting go of preconceptions and precedents.

In creative pursuits, err on the side of madness.

Instead, commercial music acts as a narcotizing force, arresting progress through its mass and heft. Rather than sounding like ♪, it sounds like $$$. Not a quarter note but a banknote.

We gorge from a virtually inexhaustible stream of contentless "content." The overdocumentation of nothingness.

A true artist suggests something more, something beyond the song. And through that they locate an indescribable, but undeniable spiritual connection with their audience—a sigh (or scream) that reaches the afterworld.

The ultimate recording device is the mind of the listener, etching sound into memory.

Neema from the Tanzania Albinism Collective reaches
for a note, fighting to find a niche of her own.

Tanzania Albinism Collective: Our Skin May Be Different, but Our Blood Is the Same

My parents
abandoned me,
because I look
the way I do.
They said I'm not
their child—
that I belong
to the "whites."

Ukerewe is the largest inland island in Africa and can only be reached by an overpacked four-hour ferry ride. It is a place so remote that historically people often traveled there to abandon their albino children

Eighteen members of the Standing Voice community volunteered for our songwriting workshop, ranging in age from twenty-four to fifty-seven. We encouraged them to write about their experiences and to express what they wanted others to understand about their existence. But even among the willing, singing out proved hard for a group that routinely avoided eye contact, rarely spoke above a mumble, and were unaccustomed to dancing.

Yet a boatload of self-serious Brooklyn shoegazers would find it a challenge to *ever* muster the unforced sorrow and despair found in the voices there. Many of the people there are burn victims from the sun, with everyday ultraviolet exposure proving life-threatening. Often at a glance they resemble the aged, and many exude a wisdom, calm, and weariness well beyond their years, a quietude found only in those who have been forced to walk on cat's paws for a lifetime.

Upon arriving, we learned that the local population with albinism had not only never been asked to sing, but often were *forbidden* to, even in church. As appalling as that is, it should maybe not come as such a surprise in light of the knowledge that even among those parents that actually do choose to keep their albino child, some still force them to eat outside and apart from their other siblings.

Not surprisingly, themes of loneliness emerged—"I Am a Human Being," "They Gossiped When I Was Born," "Life Is Hard," and "Who Can We Run To?" are just a few examples. Many lyrics were written in *Kikirewe* and *Jeeta*, both dialects which were officially discouraged following the country's unification in 1964.

It turned out that the instruments we'd sent ahead had remained untouched. So the first step was to demystify the guitars and keyboards—to have every individual hit and hold them—to introduce them as merely tools, and that rough-handling or even breaking them were permissible. They were no better than a hammer or wheelbarrow: without value unless used.

I'd learned this lesson early as a "gigging" and sometimes touring musician. I deliberately bought and played cheap instruments. Otherwise there was the handicap of putting materialism—the anxiety that you might dare scratch the exterior, etc.—ahead of freedom and creativity.

One individual on Ukerewe had found refuge at the newly built community center, after previously having lived malnourished in the bush due to being rejected by the various villages that he'd attempted to join. He subsequently engaged in repeated suicide attempts, including drinking battery acid.

Another resident shared the trauma of her repeated rapes, a horrid byproduct of the sick superstition that having intercourse with a woman with albinism was a cure for AIDS. Chillingly, Thereza detailed how in her village people often hissed "deal" when she passed—an indication of the money that her bodily parts allegedly could fetch on the underworld market.

Those who often suffer the most are the mothers who've valiantly stood by their albino offspring. Out of ignorance, husbands often accuse their wives of having cheated with a Caucasian man or they demand divorce due to their own shame. Frequently, it is an aunt or another kindhearted neighbor that takes in a rejected child as their own, assuming also the tremendous social burden that carries.

There was the thrill of playing "exotic" music for the collective and their sharing confusion that Bill Monroe was not a woman and Nina Simone and Chavela Vargas were not men. Even better was their guess that Wayo's trance music from South Sudan was from China.

While we were there, the entire island suffered an electricity blackout for more than twenty-four hours. Neither tourists nor buildings higher than a single floor are found on Ukerewe, but Maasai warrior posers are all the rage among many young men—something akin to suburban, Caucasian B-boys in America.

Witnessing the nonstop stream of people lining up to draw clean water from the well that was drilled into the heart of the albinism center had a depth of subtext—a triumph for a population that has so long been regarded as dirty and unfit.

Our last day, a village DJ set up a single hot-wired speaker. Watching over a hundred kids twerk in unison for hours—intermingling freely with members of the village was more than encouraging. It was proof that some palpable change had occurred—for the good of all—and by all hopes would continue to reverberate throughout the rising generation long after the music had died down.

Theirs is a dark, forlorn album saturated with longing and bearing a murder-ballad, goth heart. More Captain Beefheart than Ladysmith Black Mambazo, closer to DJ Screw or Alvin Lucier than most stock and stale "World Music" fare. They are more punk rock, than Prog, issuing short bursts of Morse code, distress calls from the soul.

The record features largely "found instruments"—a frying pan, sledgehammer, beer bottle and rusty nail, straw broom, and possibly the hugest kick-drum ever utilized—a ruptured rain barrel that stands taller than me and can only be encircled by six people joining hands. It radiated subs that a low-rider could die for (or *because* of).

The one trained musician in the group kept trying to control the others and interfere with their impulses, confidence, and flow, going so far as to conduct them with his arm and passive-aggressively hold back and drag the tempo, even after I'd asked them to try speeding up. Ironically, his own songs proved not as resilient as the so-called amateurs', and only one made the cut, serving as a B-side.

It is a complex and dynamic society, and as in many coastal communities there is a literal fluidity in the way life is lived—transitioning from water and land as if there is little distinction, at least for those that are fortunate enough to possess a canoe.

After the record's release, a public-radio World Music host told me he couldn't play the album because it was "too sad." It struck me that if I ever even were to have a favorite genre, it probably would be dubbed "Melancholy Music." Some of the most majestic recordings of all time are pitted with heartache.

White African Power is the name that the artists chose. It was born instantaneously out of the biggest collective improvisation (a song subtitled "We Live in Danger," only adding layers of subtext) during which there was an excess of physicality, exhilaration, and assertion. The title by design was meant to create some cognitive dissonance—they are citizens in a society where people overdose during attempts to become more alluring through skin-lightening schemes (something we also observed while in Cambodia and that Marilena herself was forced to do herself as a child in Italy) since fairer skin is seen by some as better and more desirable, but simultaneously where being *too* white can get you killed. In many ways that psychotic and contradictory ideation sums up the absurdity of prejudice and hate throughout the world.

Growing up, collective members were not allowed to play with other children, so were forced to play alone. Most were hidden when visitors came over, and their families regularly left them home if venturing out to church or the market. Therefore, many from the collective concluded that they were the only person in the world afflicted with their condition.

While spending time with the collective, it was revealed that it had always been one of the collective's standout singers, Hamidu's secret dream to sing. Unbeknownst to anyone else he would sing to himself to curb the desolation of regular abandonment—a classic case of music being medicinal.

The first time he sang in front of his peers, they burst into laughter. His shyness was so pronounced that such was their disbelief that he would sing at all, let alone so powerfully.

The desire to be heard smoldered in him so keenly that he once even saved up his meager income in order to approach the only

Elias from the Tanzania Albinism Collective tries guitar for the first time ever.

recording studio on Ukerewe Island. But despite such effort and sacrifice on Hamidu's part, the studio owner turned him away. Angrily refusing Hamidu's hard-earned shilling, the engineer shouted in Hamidu's face that he was "trash" and no one would ever want to listen to him, warning him to never return. The studio owner insisted that no matter what happened, they would never work with Hamidu.

But following the success of their debut album, *White African Power*, the members acquired passports and left their homeland for the first time ever. For some, it was their first venture off the island itself.

Once abroad, we experienced a case study in out-to-lunch paternalism. After having already been provided in writing with all of the members' names, the photographer insisted on making an illiterate artist print out her own name, which she then proceeded to laboriously misspell. This major news publication then refused to correct the verifiable error and report the artist's legal name—even when provided a scan of her passport—insisting that the information should only derive from her.

Fact-based, objective journalism at its finest.

Strikingly, when performing in Europe—a foreign land—the members noted that it was the first time that they'd ever felt that they blended in.

"We had to travel outside of our country to be heard at home."

4

We Aren't the World . . . Still! Missing Music

Imagine being from an entire country that only gets one artist promoted internationally, *ever*. A whole culture encapsulated by a lone voice, a single personality.

And that's if you're among the lucky, the chosen ones. Most nations instead remain completely unrepresented.

Envision the UK being known globally only by Cliff Richard. Nothing else. No Led Zeppelin. No Amy Winehouse. No Sex Pistols. They instead were all just destined to remain regional artists ensnared within their own territory.

Or what if the USA was repped exclusively by Barry Manilow. And Simon & Garfunkel, Frank Sinatra, Kanye West, and Patsy Cline had little choice but to be left local phenoms, due to sufficient space simply not existing for them.

Instead, quite the opposite occurs. New York, Hollywood, and London are used to leverage the rest of the world.

Worse than imbalanced demographic portrayals, we get erasures, such as when Eisenhower ordered during WWII victory parades in Paris that no black soldiers be shown, including the Senegalese who reportedly made up over half of the French riflemen—yet another complete white-out of history.

How many Hmong or Ch'ol people are there?

In such cases, size doesn't matter. If there are more than two, then you already have variety.

It's bad enough that most populations are allocated only a lone representative. But what then if the elected is a total ham like Santana?

Insult added to injury.

Try this test:

- Name three artists from Jordan? (Can you name even one?)
- Who are your three favorite singers from Indonesia?
- How's about the hottest new rapper from Zaire?

(The last question is a trick one: The nation of Zaire ceased to exist over twenty years ago.)

5

Clogged Cultural Arteries:
The Boys Are Not *Back* in
Town, They Never Left

Before written music came into being (which triggered a fracture, one that magnified even more with the invention of sound recording), any song was gone for eternity—evaporating on the very molecules that carried it—unless its melody was so contagious that it could lodge in gray matter, remain, and then gain life again atop the vocal cords of its new host.

Some songs are so ancient and inevitable (a twelve-bar Blues rag) that no one remembers or ever really knew who wrote them, they wrote themselves.

For decades now certain "classic" recordings have become vigils—never having stopped being played overlappingly at random on some radio station in the world. These are tag-teams of tyranny, a homogenizing force. Whether test dispatches to extraterrestrial life forms or mass hypnosis for those below, these standards have never been "given a rest."

6

Getting Past the Past: Pillaged Vision

In conversation, speakers used to use the word "like" as a setup to wax poetically. Now it's more often used to reference someone else's manufactured vision—a film, a book. Metaphors have even been reduced to as faint and larval a signal merely indicating an entire genre (e.g., "It was like a movie.")

In the past, people had to try to describe music rather than mimic it.

But now, musical forms have become so hackneyed that almost anyone can riff on styles like Country and Opera, easily communicating in seconds whatever they are parodying without identifying any specific song . . . and it has been this way for decades.

Genres quashed collaboration. The sad few musicians that my hometown managed to generate steadfastly refused to play together because of inflexible fiefdoms—the Prog drummer deriding the Death Metal guitarist.

Today, many people talk about media more than real life. It's safer, more distant. And instead of becoming more defined with time, reality grows more generalized.

Music doesn't die, it is eternal. But certainly it *can* stagnate.

My great-grandfather hated my grandfather's music. My grandfather my father's. And my father mine.

Folk music has progressed so little since the early 1960s that the latest, hottest indie-rock auteur would not have caused as much as a stir or double-take at a pre-Dylan hootenanny at the Cafe Wha? We are left to inhabit shells of rebellion.

What's lost is that music that doesn't progress is not "progressive." It is just a different orthodoxy.

Pop culture defanged features sheep in wolves clothing singing hot-air anthems for the devout—faked orgasm arias.

They are not the future, but the present belching fragments from the past.

I can walk by a bar in a foreign city and from just one note of an inane guitar solo know exactly what song it is, usually one recorded before I was even alive.

Musical changes used to occur mostly due to migration and wartime. But now that Western countries have stabilized, music divides more than unites as exemplified by people claiming it is "my music" rather than ours. Similar to how speaking in dialect is like throwing a gang sign, language—especially slang—is used as often to *exclude* others as it is to connect and be understood. It becomes a secret code—passwords, as it were.

The Blues today are sung as suffering on loan—an emotional hand-me-*up* to the more privileged. Rote regurgitation is not a case of "fake it 'til you make it," but until you *break* it.

Stealing another's imagination wholesale is the highest of crimes, for it is there that vision and hope are born.

It was clear to me that "rock and roll" had already lost its edge by the 1980s with the phenomenon of doctors, lawyers, accountants, and middle-school teachers forming weekend-warrior bands as pandering proof that they were still somehow quirky. This was much the same knowing but clueless wink of office-types sporting an ear-piercing as if that superficial nod lent them edge. It also smacked of the 1980s Reagan-era, doomed-for-failure aspiration to be everything and "do it all."

Today we have blueblood blondes with neck tattoos, strategically placed on the backside to enable them to be kept hidden. Being naughty for the first time has become putting your hair up rather than "letting it down."

An example of how rank things have become is a punk legend that I know who basically created a subgenre in his teens, recently confided in me that he still had "hope" because his friend's son's band had come up with a clever name. Musically, though, the youngsters were doing almost an exact replica of the music from five decades earlier, of which their dads were architects.

The result is we now have soldiers dying on battlefields in the Middle East while wailing their grandparent's music—be it AC/DC, Skynyrd, or sampled James Brown loops—groups that peaked before the current fan was even born, tunes that they were even potentially conceived to.

One of the many Abatwa villages that eerily
recall the despair of pre-casino American Indian
reservations.

Abatwa (the Pygmy): Why Did We Stop Growing Tall?

Coffee beans and gorillas—not presidents—are featured on Rwandan Francs. Nonetheless, rumor has it that select highways have been paved specifically to smooth passage for the preferred weekend getaways of the man who has singlehandedly ruled the nation since emancipating it in 1994. Fortunately for us, our route to the southwest that abuts Burundi appeared one of the chosen.

My first time stepping off of a plane in Kigali, the initial impression was confusion whether we'd touched down mistakenly in the hills of coastal northern California where I'd been raised.

In a land where men lead each other hand-in-hand, but homophobia still runs rampant, we drove off the main road and miles up the ridge just shy of the border to one of the pockets hardest hit by the genocide. It was the first place where the residents stopped waving back. It is an area so very isolated, it felt almost as if the massacre might've never ended. Topping that, we were traveling this dirt trail with two Tutsis in an area where there were recent reports of "hunting Rwandans." A sense of unrest became tangible, as if an invisible line had been crossed and we'd entered *ibiwa* ("problems").

Getting stuck crossing a stream bed, we were forced to ask directions. The dude on the tricked-out bike with "One Love, One Heart" mud flaps, said he did not know who Bob Marley was, but he professed to me that those were the words of God. In this case, the message had outlived the fame—as well it should.

Outside the village where the band declared that they were too fatigued to sing due to Malaria, residents don't have to be "taught" recycling. Every last item is reused, some purpose found. The rural population remains as it has always been, eons *ahead* of Western "progressives" in myriad ways. There, plastic bottles can lend prestige, and children clash over these remnants if cast out by passing cars, so much so that our local companions did not consider it littering. In fact, they argued that to not do so was selfish.

It was here we found the hunchback, teenage break-dancer that with his *Intore* arm-twist and foot-stomping moves, could out-battle any south Queens sidewalk challenger.

In Butare, we'd already weathered a Taylor Swift pummeling at the machine-gun guarded mall—her sound remaining sterile even when blustered through severed and tropically humidified speakers. Worse was the tag-team, lounge duo playing an off-key Reggae medley, to which the local audience straightening out the beat, clearly entrained to European 4/4 mechanical rhythms.

At the end of our meal, I stepped up onto a rickety bench to clear a restaurant urinal carelessly mounted too high for even an NBA star. It was a fixture that following installation had simply been left that way rather than corrected, made all the more striking due to the height of many in the tribe who could easily have used the bottom lip as a chin-rest.

The Abatwa ("pygmy") tribe is identified as among the most marginalized, voiceless and endangered populations in Africa. In fact, their name is frequently taken in vain as a generalized slur towards unrelated others. Still, many among their group prefer the term over the official, post-genocide, PC mouthful, replacement moniker they've been saddled with out of clear overcompensation: "The people who were left behind because of the facts of Rwandan history."

The only correct terminology is simply to call them people.

Historically, the tallest Abatwa women have attracted outside interest and then been taken as wives by other tribes. This has contributed to the physical growth of their tribe remaining limited. Though they were largely left alone during the genocide, some members of the tribe actually *participated* in committing acts of murder.

This made the hotel staff misnaming a disabled-access room the "kidnap" suite, all the more unsettling.

Far from ogling vicariously from a distance, due to Marilena's mother having lost her entire family during two earlier and less famous genocides, we live with related emotional consequences daily. We've paid respects at countless headstones, not in cemeteries, but the yards of friend's homes, often on the exact spot where the loved one(s) were felled. We've visited houses that stand abandoned, not out of fear, but despair.

And we've been led calf-deep out into the reeds where my mother-in-law's best friend's husband was last chased before being struck down in the small lake their front-porch looks out upon.

An overused phrase like, "May God bless your family," takes on a different flavor when spoken by someone whose parents and all seven siblings were massacred.

A local counseled that, "If you buy the Twa a little drink, they will dance and be happy." But plying is one piece of advice that I refuse to contemplate or obey.

The term, Cokehead was not born during the Reagan era as is commonly mistaken, but more than a hundred years before by drugged Delta mule-runners during the Reconstruction. As throughout time, anywhere people are in pain and trying to outdistance trauma, they've turned to whatever substance they could find. The times his house ran dry, my great-uncle would resort to swallowing aftershave or boil and strain shoe polish.

Intoxicated performers often feel that they are playing better, but that hardly means that they *are*. The Bob Stinson–phase Replacements were a rare exception to the rule. Live onstage, yes, substances occasionally can help a performer overcome their self-consciousness—acting as a back door to transcendence. But with recording, such disobligation routinely reveals only a lack of care.

In the hills, we were lucky enough to experience a nineteen-year-old barefoot, rookie rapper, Rosine, who is grittier than most any gangsta. And right by her side, stood, Emmanuel, the mohawk-cut traditional music master, along with a husband/wife team that trade in eerie harmonies that can make Black Sabbath sound a bit trite. Also keeping it in the family were a mother and son, Ruth Nyiramfumukoye and Patrick Manishimine, who struck dueling *Umudulis*.

When recording outdoors, trees act as resonators for wind. Therefore, a forest is the equivalent of a mountain of Marshall stacks. This presents a case where placing your back to a wall should be self-imposed. It is similar to how if defending oneself from multiple assailants, counterintuitively, being cornered limits access to your person whenever no other escape proves possible.

Another common sonic trap is a tin roof. It provides great protection. That is, until it starts raining. At that point it becomes a sound-board for the storm.

A featured instrument is the eleven-string *Inanga*, one that has a resemblance to a Boogie board and when turned upright, stands taller than some of its Abatwa players. Many of the tribe have now been consigned to government-designated villages, herded in from eons-old wandering ways. Residents claim they turn to drink due to lack of clean water. In their communities, alcoholism and depression hang thick through the air, conjuring the fractured spirit of many pre-casino-era American Indian reservations. (In the eastern Sierras, as a teenager I worked construction for a summer with my uncle. The only road in-and-out of town was edged each morning with men from their respective tribes—north or south—passed out drunk in the sun.) Paralleling elsewhere globally, corporations and rulers yearn for nomadic people to know their place and "stay put."

The recordings' reception eventually enabled touring opportunities for the group. Some were ineligible due to the inability to provide birth certificates, while others were waylaid by their addictions—too shitfaced to focus.

One member, Beatrice—a singer of effortless depth—was sixty-four-years-old before she ever was able to take a plane or venture anywhere other than Rwanda. But this was only partially true. She did leave her country once—forcibly.

When she was five years old, she was exiled into neighboring Burundi as a refugee during the first genocide (1959). Sadly though, when Beatrice was finally granted a chance, a disgruntled airline employee barred her without cause from boarding the scheduled plane, apparently due to resentment that the rural singer was experiencing such a coveted opportunity.

Her two children had toured the world as members of a government-sanctioned folkloric troupe. But it was, Beatrice, who sang uncoached and uncoaxed with a magnitude that seemed to reach forward and backwards in time simultaneously. With nothing to prove, she felt no pressure to do any extraneous thing. Every gesture

Bihoyiki from Abatwa (the pygmy) shares a
weariness well beyond her thirty-five years.

and note arrived imbued. She refused to break eye contact with me for an entire song, never once even blinking.

Similarly, Master Mong Hai in Vietnam has performed death rites for decades, singing loved one's spirits away for as long as each family felt it necessary. Oftentimes, that could be all night long or even for days at a time. Consequently, he carries a gravity and stillness that can only be earned and not learned.

Live recording is often misunderstood as a passive process. Rather than meddling, what's needed most is undivided interest and an unflagging faith in the entire endeavor's importance.

A widely held belief of ancient origins is that anything with strings or horns are instruments of the Devil. Consequently, aspiring players throughout the Deep South were left little choice but to hide their doings from parental figures. Today, a remnant of this piety that we've encountered globally are overly mannered and reverential church singers. They are living contradictions to the myth that raucous performance's genesis was black churches. This stereotype obscures that there was more of a moral tug-of-war—many parishes were forced to up their game in attempts to keep butts in the pews as secular music's popularity soared in the twentieth century. Similarly, White evangelical megacathedrals now often co-opt Nu metal guitar licks and laser-strobes into liturgies.

Historically, the Abatwa tribe were the party singers, the animators for Kings. But in our experience, it was village kids spitting freestyle verse that often packed power beyond the practiced.

A ballad "Why Did We Stop Growing Tall?" spoke quite eloquently for itself. That it was the last song recorded, hesitantly—almost as an afterthought—and one that the writer would only share in secret, made it all the more revealing.

7

The Trespass Tribe

Stockpiling songs and sounds like weapons, the West's arsenal symbolically annihilates the world and acts as an occupying force—invaders armed with guitars, laptops, and "rad" haircuts. They are aided by music's very ethereality which enables it to penetrate borders undeterred, passing where tanks and cargo could never go.

Consumerized citizens become disciplined and subjugated, the same as any good soldier, ravenously trying to buy their way back to health. And white tastes (even when regarding "black" content) remain minted as the default for rightness.

Physical isolation is a primary pitfall with interpersonal danger.

What percentage of people are jumped while looking at their phones? Or are sideswiped in crosswalks—earbuds in, literally out of synch with their environment?

So it is with culture. Instead, being heard by another is what lessens emotional burdens.

Music acts as glue—a transparent connectivity tissue that binds people together emotionally, to time and each other. But it can also divide.

Resembling seances, improvisations are hunts—for secret notes that can unlock and raise spirits, accessing another world. Though improv acts as the nuclei for all composition, it is nonetheless often looked down upon by composers with a capital "C."

As they trekked mile after mile, traditional herders practiced flutes or mouth-harps to ward off loneliness and evil spirits. Today, commuters play Ms. Pac Man on their mobiles, instead.

Historically, governments would quarantine those who were sick. Now it is the segregation itself that *makes* people ill (e.g., homeless people being confined together in close spaces and communicating disease more easily).

While recording, when musicians are baffled and isolated from one another (to the point of even being separated and staggered in time) instead of "banding" together, things routinely fall apart. Without the cohesion of proximity, unity can easily disintegrate and the likelihood of someone interrupting momentum increases—much as social obligation diminishes as barriers are introduced (e.g., callers yell and curse on the telephone in ways that almost never happen face to face. Even greater deterioration in civility follows when it comes to email/texting versus vocal encounters).

All of this rather than working towards a key musical function: to "be in tune" with one another.

Instead of window-sill, moonlit serenades of yesteryear, we get prefab song dedications—professions of love by proxy.

8

You'll Save Yourself a
Lifetime in the End

There should be no disposable places or people, no dumping grounds.

True democracy and globalization is not constituted by people buying the same brands, but the day the phrase, "I never thought it could happen here," becomes permanently displaced by, "It shouldn't happen *any*where!"

Likewise, the reflex thought when tragedy strikes, "I hope that none of _____'s family there were affected," should be struck. Distance does not lessen the tragicness.

True equity and balance could at last be mapped if ever there came a day where people no longer knew what areas to avoid to limit their susceptibility to assault. There should be no "bad" neighborhoods, only neutral—the wealth of menace and jeopardy equally shared by all.

II.

FALSE FRIENDS:

The Perils of Underestimation

9

Making a Lil' Space
for the Rest of Us

The best thing Bono could do for Africa?

Shut up.

To fall on his sword artistically (and devote to better use the millions his band lavishes overproducing tired "comeback" records—gold-plated dung).

With aging and ailing artists, it's not unlike snatching the cars keys away from ol' Granddad and taking a difficult stand, "We've all got to face it, your reflexes just aren't what they used to be. This is for the good of everyone. Especially, the children."

Or maybe what is called for more is a police command, "Please, sir, put the microphone down. *Slooooowly*. And keep your hands up where we can see them."

10

If the Truth Fits, Wear It: You Want Bigots, We've Got 'Em!

Mali has some of the worst drummers in the world.

Cuba the sorriest dancers.

Italy the worst cooks.

And no matter what color their skin, there are rednecks *everywhere*. Every culture has its own hillbillies and small-souled individuals.

Yes, they may have "jihad," but we've got "hee haw."

Every country has Country music—not Country-Western, but Country-*Far-Eastern*.

Rather than making erroneous assumptions, I live by the belief that everyone I meet is able to kick my ass *and* I never want to find out that I am wrong.

Complexion in no way correlates to aesthetic judgment. Nor does victimization guarantee and grant insight, since intellect in isolation almost always falls short.

It is emotional immaturity—unaligned hearts and minds—that we are battling. (With narcissism the polarity of empathy.) A monsoon of information will not change someone's position, unless they first soften their soul and acknowledge their own limitations, imperfections, and surrender existing *mis*-conclusions—ridding themselves of the me, for we.

And no matter how well-intended, putting someone on a pedestal in overcompensation is just a perpetuation of inequality.

Reverse reverence—not being able to see past someone's differences and through their "shit"—is still a perpetuation of bias, just another flavor of injustice and bigotry.

Clear-eyed, tough-minded, and balanced evaluation is one of the greatest gifts that we can offer any one.

More than relishing African music, I'm just as repulsed by most of it as I am Western music. The majority is just as derivative, hammy, and pathetically attention-seeking.

Reactive counter-*imbalances* aren't corrective or restorative. Someone should not be ceded the moral high-ground based solely on sexual orientation, gender, or the color of their skin (though certainly they should be actively and most carefully heard).

If it is a sham that by accidents of birth some individuals are bizarrely billionaired, then it can only also be that unfortunate circumstances do not ensure spiritual superiority. It is those with the most realized understanding that must lead, regardless of their origins.

No one is an objective expert on their own culture. We see through the limited lens of our own experience. Outsiders, though, tend to rely on overly obvious and fraudulent custodians.

Those who are unable to ignore someone's otherness and recognize that person's individual flaws, inadvertently engage in discrimination, continuing it in an altered form. Excessively PC vigilantes wind words into nooses, cinching them off from meaning.

Trauma does not guarantee insight. It only renders it more likely. It is the truth that deserves to stand before convenient narratives.

There is an unspoken privilege to being first and, at the opposite end, inheritors. But being gay and/or female alone is a start, not a finish. Politics or identity *du jour* is insufficient to sustain interest and ends up detrimental due to the backlash it creates, causing a disservice to other more worthy peers that will henceforth be denied a fair hearing.

Any artist—no matter where they are from—should be admired only sincerely and with equity, never charitably. Such attentions are just another lie.

11

More than We'll Ever Know:
Watch Out for the
Little Stuff

Overtly political music has had far less societal impact than banal music.

Sadly, the Devil almost always has a better soundtrack.

Good intentions and just causes alone are simply not enough. Songs must stand on their own, the music speak for itself. A compelling backstory is not enough. Without the beats to justify the posturing, releasing such a record is actually counterproductive, leading listeners to grow even more cynical.

The starkest damage tends to come not from immorality, but *amorality—s*ystems that operate only for profit, without care for consequences or sustainability.

Survival is dependent on a few core elements and instincts: food, sex, fight-or-flight, music, religion. People are widely willing to experiment living without religion. But not without music, not absent some spirituality of however vague and amalgamous a sort.

If tested, I hazard to "guess" that neurologically someone is working harder—benefitting more—while listening to John Coltrane's complexities than, say, vacant fare like Mariah Carey. And when it comes to an artist like Elliott Smith, emotions are more engaged, as opposed to full-on, adolescent aggro music that by design stimulates the reptilian stem, not introspection.

Akin to food that delivers calories with no nutrition, music without depth blocks the arteries of the culture's circulatory system.

Some of the people I love and respect most eat horribly or suffer from addiction, or both. Similarly, many of them have pedestrian tastes in music. None of this interferes with my esteem for them, though. Instead, it only makes me pine that they could be more profoundly enriched by music.

Patient to Take Him Whole, the Hurt Lay in Wait for Him His Entire Life

I was left to wonder what my uncle would sound like if he ever trusted himself enough to sing. At age thirty-six, lost for eternity was the chance to truly hear him and share a higher level of connection. I only know that if he'd ever tapped the world of pain inside of him, it could have rocked stadiums.

Greg was not my only aunt or uncle struggling with addiction. But he was the only one with an undetected defective aorta, just waiting to blossom inversely. It only took the right dose of cocaine and heroin to rip the life from his chest vertically, top to bottom.

Buzzed on misprinted Coors cans his factory had discarded, he'd turn me on to sounds beyond my immediate world—*Led Zeppelin II*, the Grateful Dead's *American Beauty*. They were hash-resin stained gatefolds that hinted at something more.

Clapping his hands and stomping feet, he always rushed the beat. He'd hold out his arm and flex his bicep for me to feel.

"I've been working out. Can't you tell?"

It was the first of many lies—questions that weren't really questions, but pleas.

At least for a few minutes now I can still close my eyes, listen, and you are here again with me.

If I could sing you back to life I would—to the place where it all just becomes a single hymn.

The sound floor for recording Afar singer Yanna
Momina was literally the ocean tide.

Afar Ways:
Raising the Dead
on the Red Sea

We were seated high on the floor of a stilt hut when the tide came in fast, flanking us. The band's sound waves rode atop ocean waves, the floor rocking in the current.

The beach entrance's walls brimmed with broken bottles, provisional barbed wire. On the opposite side, local boys had cleared a soccer field in the dump, using mounds of trash for goalposts. Their teeth were sharpened to points, as is the custom.

And the ridgeline above looked like it had been bitten. Beneath it, the underground Chinese military's only overseas base was lodged cavernously into the hillside.

Making music is not something the rural Afar people do for show, the quartet told us. Since most have no television, it is done for their own amusement at night. *Every* night.

Smoking Camel cigarettes in the desert land where camel meat is a delicacy, we huddled beneath a second story that was held up more by chance than plywood.

Djibouti is not a "developing country." All countries are developing—for better or worse. Instead, Western nations have *over*-developed, petulantly refusing to scale back for the sake of the whole. Here, they didn't make the cars smaller. They just never got big.

Seventy-one-year-old Yanna was discovered while accompanied on a two-string shingle played with nails along with matchboxes for maracas. She made a name for herself not just for her kamikaze vibrato but also for being the rare Afar woman who writes her own songs.

To my surprise, she danced as I was tuning but then ceased when I began to actually play.

Moving at the speed of another culture, what first sounded like a call to prayer was only conversation.

And then we began.

We recorded quickly. More recording time generally just allows for more time to potentially fuck things up.

As an experiment, I asked her to try speaking over some music. On the spot she brainstormed a septuagenarian rap for the ages, riding an imaginary bassline for over ten minutes that could be felt though not heard.

Then, after a manic burst of tunes, she asked her band to set down their instruments and undertook an *a cappella* rendition of "My Family Won't Let Me Marry the Man I Love (I Am Forced to Wed My Uncle)," a song that the others had never heard before.

It was followed by a wordlessness that made it undeniably clear that our recording had concluded.

You Can Have It All for a Song

A voice is the face of the sound.

A producer's task is to find the heart of a song, the center, to help clear away the sludge around to bring better clarity to the narrative. To disappear into the music, so all that is left is the song.

I am interested in process, not product. I try not to consider myself at all. Pop culture has a tendency towards grandiosity. But the reality is that today's "hip" and *avant-garde* is tomorrow's quaint. And almost all "superstars" will soon be forgotten. They are destined as future footnotes, at best.

Songs need tension and release, reflecting all lifeforms' oscillation. In order to free ourselves from predictability's pull, we must swim across, not against the riptide.

Fully realized records invoke the visual as much as aural— arousing a multisensory experience.

A great song should feel like being shot with the reverse of a bullet. It instead extracts something injurious from your person.

The point of a song is to try to live your life onwards as impassioned as those three minutes made you feel—to capture photos that are films, single lines that are novels, and folk songs as symphonies.

My goal is not to preserve anything. The purest experience is witnessing a sound being born for the first time. Rather than mimicry, the nobler quest is to make noises that few, if any, have before beheld. If such is not the quest, then why bother to pile more redundancy atop the clutter?

Paradoxically, my role is not to change any artist but to help them sound *more* like themselves.

Musicology is interested in death—trying to preserve something before it perishes. I am interested in the opposite end of the spectrum, the creation of something that otherwise would not have occurred if the process itself hadn't acted as a midwife.

Music's destiny is freedom.

Before the Middle Ages, there were no bar lines at all. Then the music was broken up, imprisoned into brittle approximations that leveled disfiguring violence upon the actual sounds that the written transcriptions were designed to depict. Vietnam veteran and Free Jazz stalwart Butch Morris conducted musicians in an intuitive and impressionistic way rather than a formalized one, restoring a floating sensation, rising like apparitions.

When music went vertical with harmonic development in Medieval churches, overall it stopped moving linearly, and related further forward progress became blocked. Any new twist also brings adhesions—precedents and no longer as clean of slate.

We don't need to tweak music with dials and processors. It arrives pre-tweaked by whatever its environment—the material that composes the surrounding four walls, the ceiling's height, the region's humidity, etc.

The best bits of artistic expression are prisoners sprung, fugitives making a mad dash for the gate. Knowing full well that they'll be shot in the back, never making it through, still they run as fast as they can. For as long as that stretch lasts, there is a taste of liberation.

Music at its strongest is a form of time travel. The healthiest art echoes and plants seeds elsewhere—building a future, rather than leeching off of the past.

12

Hyphens & Fingerpaint:
Art without Heart

Combinatory creativity is the basest level of art. The majority of pop music is the result of just such mix-and-match, hyper-hyphenation. When quality ingredients are lacking, radical combinations are used to compensate. It is the opposite of purity.

The dominant genre is not even Retro music but Stagnant sounds. For Retro would be reviving something that went away, not continuing to indulge what refuses to relent and perpetually remains. Instead we are left with hindsight-visioned prophets and subjected to emotional adolescents trafficking in store-bought pain.

This is "comfort music"—meatloaves of sound.

It is nostalgia masquerading as innovation, that instead vaguely or explicitly conjures up someone or something familiar from the relatively recent past.

Corporations frack culture and the backlog is so grave that the delay in innovation reaching the masses is ever prolonging. Punk hit with the Ramones in 1976 but didn't enter the mainstream until fifteen years later with Nirvana's breakthrough. Hip Hop was arguably born in the South Bronx with the Ghetto Brothers in 1971, but it took another fifteen years for a crossover hit with "Walk This Way" and only then by riding the coattails of an ailing arena-rock band. After that, it still took more than thirty years for Rap to topple rock and become the top-selling genre in America.

Almost nobody will voluntarily be listening to fluff artists a decade on from their peak. But nonetheless they will be forced to hear them repetitively via commercialized broadcast systems.

Commercialized culture loves the trappings but not what's inside—all filler, no killer. Fashion designers have long trolled the backstreets for trends, but when it comes to musical forms, they're usually adopted by name alone. *The Jazz Singer* was the first "talkie" film (1927) but had nothing to do with jazz. Even worse, it featured Al Jolson doing blackface. Bing Crosby starred in *Birth of the Blues* in 1941, which could just have easily been labelled *Death of the Blues* as it featured the crooner known for playing priests and starring in *White Christmas,* aptly enough.

As the buyer for one of the last remaining record retail chains told me recently, "The only thing that sells anymore are dead people."

13

Wormholes

In Sicily, I watched a goth woman—shrouded in sunglasses and kerchief—ride her beach cruiser deliberately slow, winding through the cobblestone streets every day with a boombox propped in her handlebar basket and roaring the same 1980s hair metal songs at the precise time each morning, as if caught in a wormhole. It was simply sepulchral. Through her, the band Poison lived on, poisoning the city streets with fourth-grade English and bombast.

Now with the internet, nothing gets fully metabolized, never quite going away completely.

Often, one-hit wonders resemble more inverted demonic possessions, channeling a lone song that bears no relationship to anything that person ever uttered before or after. But in these cases, it is not an evil force speaking through them, but some divinity far more inspired than they.

The line of suffering between guards and inmates
at Zomba Prison is often a fuzzy one.

Zomba Prison Project: I Will Not Stop Singing

In music freedom can be found that is otherwise unavailable. "When we're singing the walls are no longer there, I forget that I am in prison. But when we stop, the walls return. And we're back counting the bricks again."

Following the release of the first Zomba Prison Project record, Malawi slipped to the number-one poorest nation on earth. This has been evidenced at the prison itself by inmates going three full days without eating due to "delayed funding" from the government, breaking the all-too-frequent one- or two-day stints. We only discovered this when making a surprise visit to the prison while we were en route back to the airport, an experience akin to returning home unannounced after having just left for work and finding your spouse in the shower with the next-door neighbor.

Over time, we were able to see many of the men and women gain release, gradually shedding prison from their system, but never quite fully shaking it. Spiking the good news, though, two female inmates whose cases we first appealed in 2013 remain incarcerated as a result of their files having been "lost." This means that they are being held without any documentation whatsoever as to why. And another inmate, Elube—whose charges we also were having actively reviewed—perished in the prison, as her own child had done the year prior to the recording of the first album.

That Zomba Prison Project debut album received the first Grammy nomination ever for Malawi, an honor that more than 80 percent of African nations have not yet gained. Welcomingly, worldwide media swarmed to Zomba Prison as a result. Sadly though, many "journalists" failed to delve too deeply into the facts, instead only interviewing, filming, and photographing prisoners from the male band, most of whom had nothing at all to do with the nominated record. Worse yet, the global media almost wholeheartedly ignored the women, whose contributions had made up more than *half* of the songs.

Similarly, a kind donation was made providing additional equipment to the already outfitted men, whose practice room then became piled ceiling-high with amps à la Motörhead or Spinal Tap. Meanwhile, the women remained with nothing but a single hand-drum (... and they were forced to share even that meager instrument half of the time with the men)

We were saturated by waves of sour grapes from urban music scenesters in Malawi who claimed that there were much better artists in the country—often meaning *themselves*—who should be receiving acclaim instead of Zomba Prison. No doubt those they were championing were better schooled. But extrapolating from this logic would mean that all nineteen million plus Malawians were by birth preset with greater artistic insight than any outsider could ever possess, that all of our artistic fates were predestined.

Even though the leader of Zomba's male band, Binamo's, repeatedly protested that it was "impossible" to write a song in mere days per our request, on our last morning at the prison he pulled out as riveting of a plea as can be found, "I Will Never Stop Grieving for You, My Wife." It came replete with orchestrated handclaps. From the first note, my breath thinned as I feared anything might interfere with such a miraculous unveiling. Then in the distance at the entry gate, a car horn was tooted. But rather than ruin such a resplendent take, it only enhanced it, with more splendor than anything that could've been planned.

People with poor boundaries are attracted to prisons—places where there are clear-cut limits and lines, rife with oversimplified, dichotomized roles: good guys/bad guys.

The commissioner disturbingly relished describing a past prison rape initiation where a makeshift quartet of men in drag, mimicked absent instruments with their mouths—guitar, bass, drums. The new arrivals were then awakened during the night and paraded into this bizarre, handheld lighter-lit scene.

The angelic-voiced Elias serves life at Zomba Prison.

I've traveled to the top of Zomba Mountain, where transatlantic, hand-me-down Rolling Stones stocking caps are worn only for the warmth that they provide. When asked, the four generations of men said they didn't know the meaning of the lips-and-tongue logo.

(And, this is not so different than in Paris where I met a preteen youngster wearing a *Dark Side of the Moon* T-shirt because she "thought it looked cool," but had no clue who Pink Floyd was or that the logo was even associated with music.)

This harkens back to a kid from the village who almost got his ass kicked by some football hooligans in the UK for wearing the faded T-shirt of a rival team that he was wholly unaware of.

And it is soccer players—if anyone—that are famous worldwide, not pop stars.

Do many of the Zomba mountain men know who Messi is?

Yes.

But Ed Sheeran or Madonna?

Hell no!

Nor is 9/11 on most radars, an event which simply mirrors similar (or greater) levels of suffering that their own regions have lived or live currently, sometimes over the span of generations.

Home Is Where the Hurt Is:
A Tragicomedy in Two Acts

Few people can sing with as much pathos as my bipolar grandfather did. He mangled shabbily recalled Irish standards that his own father had smuggled over and shared only when intoxicated.

Like so many immigrants, my grandfather's father had wanted to forget the homeland. It was his offspring that were determined to bring it back to life, in however misshapen and *under*-understood a form.

My great-grandfather had left Ireland as a teenager with his only surviving family member, his younger brother. Landing at Ellis Island, they worked the railroads, slowly snaking their way across the states. He eventually threw down roots amid the plains of Utah, where Irish Catholics were regarded as riffraff by the Mormon majority and forced to settle on the wrong side of the tracks.

And so his brother continued onwards to San Francisco, smacking up against the edge of the Western world, and then eventually drowning there in the bay. The official family story was that my great-uncle had been a "swim champion" who died during a tournament. In reality, he was schizophrenic and had heaved himself overboard a ferry, only to surface days later, waterlogged, a John Doe—laid to rest in an unmarked, pauper's grave.

Immeasurable generations have tried to shore up the dam on migration—the Protestants hating the Irish and Italian people, the Irish and Italians then turning on African-Americans heading north and west, trading agricultural life for urban opportunity. And all resistance has proven futile. We move by nature.

My own grandfather's hands trembled so badly from lithium that he would spill nearly half of every glass he drank to take his pills. He was forced to lower his head to drink rather than bringing the water to his lips, and still he slopped most over the sides. Doctors claimed he was part of the drug's first trial, during its earliest experimental phase.

I am haunted by the why he carried perennially in his eyes.

He'd run an obstacle-course life—a series of wrong turns and impasses.

He forgot most everything—car keys, birthdays—and called his own children with interchanged names. The unwavering clarity of his machine-gun mind, though, was remembering bits from the "homeland" that he'd never really known.

They sent her home to die. Because that's what they did during that era. She had a hole in her heart (and still does), but she survived, and even thrived.

Our town was almost entirely lacking in diversity, and people with disabilities were still shuttered and rarely seen. Based on the most common reactions, my sister may as well have been Ziggy Stardust. This was years before mainstreaming was even thought of.

But though Jane is nearly nonverbal, she is multilingual. She knows the words to almost every song. She just joins in and makes them up as she goes along.

Similarly, not yet two years of age, my daughter would point from my forehead to her own repeatedly. Then from her heart to my chest and back. These solemn repetitions spoke more eloquently than any words I've heard.

If any choreographer is lost for inspiration, they need not scour Philly sidewalks or Rio de Janeiro favelas. They'd be well served to heed the freedom found in Down Syndrome dance. Never have I seen more unselfconscious bodily expression than at Friday night rec-center DJ nights with my older sister and her peers.

As a teenager I worked weekends at a developmental disability center. The same Top 40 band had come there every weekend for as far back as anyone could recall. I started instead hosting cream-of-the-crop, original-music bands from the local scene. Though road-tested and club-headlining bands, they nonetheless invariably said that is was on these weekend nights that they found the most appreciative audience they'd ever played for.

One glam band held as a highest honor that their music had obliterated the record for the number of residents sent to their rooms for "stimulations," the quasi-scientific euphemism for masturbation.

One man, Tom's trademark was as singular a move as I've ever witnessed. This was despite or maybe in part because of its utter simplicity—holding his palms lackadaisically above his head, rotating his torso side to side, and flopping his wrists in circles like a grand marshal atop a motorcade. But identical to all embodied art, the poignancy of it can never be recreated or described, only experienced. Similarly, outsiders cannot reproduce Italian hand gestures deftly since they miss the underpinning subtle kaleidoscope that lies *beyond* the hands. The expressions are incomplete without involving the entire arm, body, voice, mouth, and brow, elements that are almost impossible to embody unless immersed in them from birth.

I cannot capture the power of Tom's dance, any more than it is possible to explain an Isadora Duncan twirl or a Marlon Brando stutter.

Capoeira, the Brazilian discipline, is often promoted as a self-defense system disguised as dance and descended from slaves. But all dance is ultimately an act of self-preservation, moving our way out of, through, or toward something.

14

Mineral Deficiency

As a species, we were actually healthier physically as hunter-gatherers. Once we began farming, our diet became more stable but less varied.

And so it is with corporate media content.

Capitalism has even managed to tame bebop's anarchy into wallpaper—played, but no longer heard. Jazz that once was so shocking that you couldn't *not* listen to it serves today as background Muzak at airport cafés and boutiques—revolution rendered invisible and disappeared. History doesn't have to be rewritten if no one reads it, and revolutionary sound need not be banned if it is being ignored.

Many people claim they listen to "everything," but quite the contrary is true. What they are exposed to has been manipulated and narrowed, shiftily segregated into marketing slots.

With the internet, algorithms feed people back ever attenuated recommendations, reinforcing rather than widening their tastes. And with one click, dubious playlists are tipped to hundreds of thousands, instead of passed mouth to ear like state secrets across a record store counter.

As the music becomes tamer, the outfits and haircuts grow more frenzied. We are subjected to "personalities" with little personality—screeching battle cries for nothing, asphyxiating moshpits of mediocrity.

15

The Easter Bunny, Superstars, and Further Fairy Tales

Established artists should be held to a higher standard than others, not a lower one. The same as an automobile driver may bear a greater degree of legal liability than a cyclist, and an adult more than the child. With power comes greater responsibility.

Instead, fans customarily grow overly charitable and fawning when it comes to superstars.

But idol worshipping is one of the least rebellious actions possible, even if that figure is pseudo-rebellious (or maybe *especially* so when that's the case). It is misapplied and convoluted affection, like feeding pigeons that infest cities or regarding poisonous pet pythons as "sweet."

The failing of most revivalists is that they are overly reverential despite the musical form they worship having stemmed from irreverence—a necessity for any new musical movement to emerge.

When people are invested and want somebody to be good, the performers do not have to *be* good. They just have to avoid being overly bad. Their evaluation is made through rose-colored lenses.

This is the bias that results in "He's really talented," which is just an upgrade from "He doesn't totally blow."

Those of us from the industrialized, right-brain world generally have been wound tight by our culture. Locked in a bar-arm hold, but refusing to say "give!," far too many—if they even brave a dance floor—shimmy stiffly as if trying to shake themselves unfrozen.

Immigrant Song:
The Refugee Rock Stars

It was easier to score drugs than find music at the refugee camp.

We'd traveled to France's northern coast—the section American troops stormed in WWII, the area where the British fought one of their ugliest battles and over a hundred thousand people perished. It is a land beaten to shit, by wars and the elements.

Coinciding by chance with our trip, the infamous "jungle" migrant camp in Calais—the last stop before passage to the UK—was being dismantled. Truckloads of stoic French police stood by like jailers. The tents and plywood shacks had spread, filling the gaps between the twenty-five-foot-high fences surrounding the Chunnel's entrance. It was an upside-down penitentiary, designed to keep people out rather than in.

The night we arrived there, a teenager had died beneath the wheels of a semi. Tiring as he lay supine, clinging to the chassis, he let go just shy of reaching Britain.

A former teacher with four children offered to give us one of her offspring, "Here, want to take her?" She was half-kidding, but that only made it more sinister. At chest level, she clenched both fists and then opened them languidly while making a plosive sound with her mouth to enact how her husband had died by way of a Syrian landmine.

The camp was almost 100 percent men, most under age thirty. The majority milled lethargically or sat idle and sullen, smoking. The NGO and aid workers had flooded in from across the Western world, creating a strange degree of privilege amid the squalor. The aura of many of the college-aged do-gooders resembled concierges at fancy-pants hotels more than social workers—almost forcing food, clothing, and care packages upon all comers, whether desired or not.

The resulting entitlement was reflected in the attitude of some residents. One musician refused to play for us because "I just got done doing a phone interview with CNN. And I am speaking with the BBC later today." He said it with the grandiose weariness of a budding Silverlake indie-film starlet at the end of a long day's press junket. More than one stood us up at the predetermined meeting time.

Most tellingly, a young shyster with a quarter-note pendant necklace and hundred-dollar haircut oozed rock star attitude, keeping us waiting for over an hour, though he was just a few football fields away, and then arriving with a full posse in tow. He declared impatiently, "How can I help *you*? I'm very busy right now." His forearms were stacked with silver-bracelets he wore like bohemian military stripes, every gesture accentuated by the rattle. He was his own best accompanist.

I inquired whether he wrote songs. This propelled him into a five-minute diatribe about the required process for songwriting. This was his defense as to why he had never copped a single tune. He demonstrated the hallmark trait of any narcissist: there was a clear trade-deficit interpersonally—not once did he show any interest in who we might be or have to offer.

These dwellings were putrid places where people had been stopped, stuck at a geographic edge. But in defiance of my expectations, I came to realize that often the migratory path acts as a filter, an inversion of natural selection—survival of the *un*-fittest. As reluctant as I am to acknowledge this, the more savvy and resilient from their homelands had already cunningly found a way through or welcomed any haven (rather than stubbornly holding out for a preconceived preference, as many here had—"I don't want to remain in France, I want to go to England" was a common complaint). Or those had stayed home and stood their ground, risking life and limb defending their nation and people.

There is music everywhere. But it is given birth by the willing. This was one of the rarefied places where we were left empty-handed.

Sadly, the whole camp burned to the ground a year later following a brawl between Afghans and Kurds. Fifteen hundred souls ended up homeless *again*, this time on a different continent, one that they'd trekked so far—many on foot—to reach as they sought some sort of refuge and peace.

She was shot through the face. It came to light later that it had been a policeman's bullet. She was only two years old.

Her crime? Being born into a migrant family. Fleeing war, the toddler was instead eventually held prisoner in a "peaceful" country during a high-speed chase with human traffickers at the wheel. Careening, the drivers even held her out of the van's window as a threat at one point.

The trauma rippled through the community and our second attempt to record in Calais crumbled (It was already teetering due to the nightly raids and razing of encampments).

In the days prior, we had recorded with a few folks.

I learned long ago that the seemingly shy one almost never is. The leader was so strikingly starry-eyed—I knew he was either an artist or schizophrenic. It is such a fine line between the two.

He greeted the instrument with the awkward, ham-handed, out-of-tune, open-string guitar strum that is a dead giveaway of someone who has never held it before.

I could sense he wasn't long for this world. Twenty or thirty years, if that. Not even a lifetime. But that span is mere seconds if you keep fucking up doing the same shit.

Due to the influx of NGOs, the camps are likely the only place that you will behold homeless so pampered that they refuse a warm meal if it is not to their liking.

Volunteers reach near shoving matches determining who will help whom. The region's surplus is much like soup kitchens on Christmas morning when do-gooders have to be turned away, despite the programs' desperately low supply of help the remainder of the year.

The Objective?
Objectivity

Once I'd finally given up on my own aspirations as an artist I made it my duty to dutifully record bands I *didn't* like. The intention was to actively try to find something about even that music that I could relate to. Similarly, as a music journalist writing for local papers, I attempted to highlight anything that was unique, even if it wasn't my thing. I wrote about any artist who was doing something distinguishable rather than good imitations of petrified material.

Valuable distinctions for me are not good/bad, but honest/phony and idiosyncratic versus staid.

Not smart versus dumb, but (*slightly* more) objective versus biased and tampered.

It was watching songwriter Vic Chesnutt play his first West Coast show ever that tilted my trajectory towards becoming a producer. By blind luck, my so-so band shared a bill with him. But we didn't deserve to be in the same room. As I witnessed Vic unveil his music, it was undeniable how effortlessly he reached heights I'd never be able to, no matter how furiously I tried.

Tragically, Vic overdosed on painkillers Christmas morning more than a decade later, distraught by mountains of medical bills.

I desire to participate in bringing things into the world that would otherwise not exist. Singularity over technical "goodness" is the determining factor. What else is the point, except to add more to the excess? Authorship does not matter nearly as much as a creative experience and *any* proof of its existence.

Marilena and I enter every project with a complete willingness to *not* release it, should it not meet the above criterion (as evidenced by the many field-recording stories here that have not culminated in records). Thus, we have refused to participate in multiple paying projects and have shelved adequate but unremarkable music.

The goal is to get the ego out of the art. Anything less easily becomes the equivalent of a musical selfie.

In hindsight, I can see that all of my own bands sucked.

The main reason was that they always had at least one member who was an accidental asshole.

Me.

III.

MUSIC MATTERS:

The Trivial Should
Not Be Trivialized

16

Anti-depressing

A microphone acts as a confessional for atheists.

Follow your heart and it will lead you places your mind can never find, or reach.

A guitar is nothing if not a compass, it can help locate the way, which direction to go. It remains the most reliable therapist I've known.

Music is psychiatric—frequencies wash over and alter our neurology. It reorganizes our psyche, metabolizing experiences—acting as an X-ray of the soul.

People often relate that music is like a drug.

But it's not only "like a drug." It *is* a drug, unlocking the chemistry and potential already inside of us.

Art is capable of helping make someone a better person, but not by reinforcing vanity (e.g., "Me music"). It can only do so through the humility that inescapably emerges whenever someone becomes more sensitized to the world around them.

The secret ingredient in cooking and music is always love—not of self, but for others.

In helping outstrip oneself, art fulfills its highest function.

17

Don't Believe Half of What You See, but (*Almost*) Everything You Hear

Sonics are the most supernatural art form, as they produce no object. Unlike sculpture, music is not a thing, but an experience.

Recording, though, turned music from an activity into something material. Later, promotional music videos emerged, rendering visual what had been a strictly aural experience. This has now led to the phenomenon of people often watching videos on mute, completing the cycle of divorcing sound *from itself*.

The commercial has become the show.

These "music" clips that once sold songs now instead are born from songs that sell image.

Sound is vibration. It literally makes the air quake, causing something that we can't see to move.

The ultimate loss of musicality in speech is silence, which we have largely fallen to in front of machines and screens.

But even deaf people can hear. In WWI, doctors had a test for malingering deserters. Those that claimed they heard nothing at all were immediately sent back to the frontlines. The experts knew that the truly shell-shocked remained able to sense some vibrations from the tuning fork despite their hearing loss.

For the majority of species, listening carefully is a matter of life and death, else they become prey. Instead, for many of us, our most intimate relationships languish due to inattention.

18

Art Super-sized

Nick Drake could never have dreamed how many babies would be made to his suicide serenades. The official claim is that he had not left a goodbye note. Clearly they weren't listening closely enough to his songs. Every line was a cry for help, an awkward, extended farewell.

But just because an artist's recognition comes long overdue—even posthumously—doesn't guarantee that phase might also only be a fad, and that they will shed into obscurity yet again.

Supreme artists do not perform genres.

Billie Holiday did not play Jazz. She played herself, her entire lifetime. She was a conduit, her heart expanding to fill and reach all of the places that her conscious mind couldn't. She went so deep inside a song, she never quite came all the way back.

Jimi Hendrix was not a rock musician or a traditionalist. He was a futurist, an anomaly unleashing before-unheard torrents of noise.

They were archangels who did not necessarily care much of God.

Output is not based on input. This is the lie that capitalism spreads, that anything can be had potentially through proper consumption.

But I could dutifully listen to all of the same music as Miles Davis, wear identical clothes, ingest the same drugs, retrace his exact steps and postures. And still I would not even come within a galaxy of sounding as mutedly mesmeric as he.

The more people rely on external sources, the more limited and redundant the resulting musical output.

What will become of cultures when all memory is externalized? Originality entails purposeful forgetting, shedding the past so that fresh sinew can materialize.

The sorcery of art and ideas is that something *can* come from nothing. And that thing is often much better than anything which existed before.

Watching my daughter as a toddler, it is readily apparent that her behavior is not entirely imitation, but inspiration. Many behaviors arise from inside her, from somewhere else, unseen.

People are not usually lastingly changed by events but by process. The day-to-day investments that build or whittle away at one's body, psyche, or soul.

End World Hunger Day?

What a well-intentioned but wholly unrealistic vision.

"*Minimize* World Hunger Day" or "*Reduce* Starvation Now" are far less catchy, but potentially achievable goals.

Like "world peace," these are not quagmires that we can fix once, wash our hands of, and be finished with forever. They require vigil and maintenance. The world has never been at peace—just certain regions, during select intervals, at best.

A million people can march on Washington and give rousing speeches. But within days they are metabolized by the nine-to-five grind, the stock market's hacked-out grooves.

Things change sustainably not from grand gestures, but micro-commitments.

Timeless artists defy the historical gravity of trends. They offer expressiveness as distinctive as fingerprints. But more often we are left with parasitic, overly tutored voices that act as spores.

Ineffable performances eclipse the concept of competition. There is no better-than. They simply are, their power palpable. The most infectious dance rhythms act as puppet strings, the beat pulling people to their feet, making their skeletons move and slipping them into a groove that illuminates precisely where each step should go.

Put Your Music Where Your Mouth Is

A pop song asks the vital question: How do you want to spend the next three minutes of your life?

Timeless songs offer a promise of escaping yourself, a temporary oasis.

Like premonitions, they act as CPR for the spirit, able to revive the (nearly) dead. Lifetimes pass between us in those moments.

Artists should invest more of themselves into each note rather than compulsively adding yet more notes to the stew.

The most important instrument is the body. Everything else is an extension of it.

Seek out knock-kneed rhythms, for music without countermotion and cross-currents is like a sketch without any shading or use of perspective.

Cardboard-cutout singers seem as if they have never sung for anyone but themselves. And Autotune is like doping in sports. It props up pitch-corrected, gutter-guard singers. To paraphrase a biblical passage, if one speaks in the tongues of men and angels, but without love, it is only a resounding gong, an empty and clanging cymbal.

Silence is only generalized noise masking what is deemed "sound."

Empathy is to truly hear someone. Perhaps even more closely than they can hear *themselves*.

19

Autopsies on a Ghost

The beauty of a record is that the listener(s) it might most impact may not even be born yet and could potentially listen for the first time long after the artist has left this world. This influence can even occur transgenerationally, without any direct inheritance, but instead leap-frogging over decades to land—at long last finding a home, however ephemeral.

How many people attended the first reading of the epic poem *Howl*? The estimate runs around 150 people, tops. But it's easy to argue that 1955 October night in San Francisco eventually altered the world socially.

Can mere numbers measure the success of such things, the power of messages that strengthen with time?

Women accused of witchcraft are left homeless and risk death by sticks and stones should they ever attempt to return to their village.

Witch Camp (Ghana):
I've Forgotten Now
Who I Used to Be

Google moved their AI here, little doubt unhindered to experiment in ways not allowed in the States. But we were days north from that take-over—the urban pockets of prosperity, capitalistic cosmetics for all intents and purposes.

The side roads to the rural hotels are dotted with smug sex-tourists trailed by resigned and bereft young "girlfriends."

"There is no need to travel to Accra for God. He is already *here*," a radio prophet ranted, followed by a praising singer baptized "Elvis." This godly place is where elderly women are exorcized through force-feedings of chicken blood, monkey skulls, and mud.

They are believed cured if they survive this concoction for seven days, but one would think that quite the opposite would prove truer.

Those declared "witches" survive selling firewood. Or they work the field for the chiefs. Some are forced into prostitution. Albeit rarer, there are also men accused, and they are deemed "wizards."

But the only demons most of these women are in touch with are their own. Their mental health issues and their physical ailments—blindness, misshapen limbs—rather than inspiring compassion have instead been vilified, and the vulnerable shunned and ostracized, usually as a ruse to steal their land after their husband's passing.

Ghana hosts one of the key ports where countless communities and families were torn apart during America's slave trade. Today, cruelty continues in a retooled form.

Victims are blamed to provide emotional distance and a greater sense of difference than exists. Right here in our supposedly "post-feminism" era, the persecution of alleged witches still endures. Some are marked with tribal facial scars given at birth, others as part of their banishment. It is yet another regional twist on how the world manages to persecute women.

It took five planes to get there, where the road ends, down by the riverbed. It's not just a shoeless place, but pantless. If you can't afford diapers, it makes sense to simply not have your children wear anything at all, waist down.

Back at our lodge, the electric water heater had not been properly grounded, and hence required risking your life for a shower—cleanliness next to deadliness, as it were.

A Ghanaian acquaintance from the capital shot video on his phone like a tourist. He laughed that he'd never seen five people on a single motorbike before. But then, within a block, it happened again—this time it was a father with what looked like quadruplets but were simply sisters descending closely in age. They rode like surfers on land.

Bearing black plastic sacks of kola nut offerings for the kings as is custom, the driver first took us to the wrong village on purpose. Then, after recognizing our determination and sincerity about who we desired to meet, he acquiesced, and we began to search in earnest.

As so often, the main obstacle in communication was neither a lack of hearing nor misunderstanding of facts, but an absence of belief in the message. There is routinely an adjustment before others accept, "Oh, *that's* what you're looking for?" rather than steering you towards what they thought you meant.

With complex problems there are no villains, but many small heroes. The mostly elderly women have been exiled, with the threat of murder if they dare return home. Not so differently, Americans commit their parents to convalescent homes.

But aside from the official witch camps, a few kind chiefs secretly shelter the shunned.

One such chief told me, "I thought I was the only one. Now, with you, we are two. Anyone who honors God cares for these women first— those who are persecuted."

This was answered with the king's groupies signature snap authenticating membership, a double-jointed dragging of the thumb across the entire palm, popping like Roman candles. The king lives indoors beside his white stallion, a stud grazing on hay and pissing torrents beside the tribal throne.

This king is reportedly the best farmer in the region. It is often forgotten that locals were kidnapped not just for their labor, but their technology. They were experts at growing the crops that their future southern-state masters were profiting from but had not a clue how to cultivate.

We brought a famous local musician along to record one day, but he struggled to keep pace with the villagers and find space musically. On a break between takes, a preteen sat down uninvited at the hot-shot's instrument and tried playing for the first time ever. The notes that flowed out of him with intuitive ease were mind-bendingly original. I felt a shudder as the novice toyed with chaos, but never quite succumbed. The master musician tensed, undeniably outmatched.

Almost as penance, in the car on the way home we were subjected by him to Celine Dion duetting with Sinatra's ghost.

The challenge is to transcend pride. The difference with first-time, first-impulse musicians is that their ego does not usually need to be overcome since it is rarely a factor to begin with. With stars, though, if vanity even were not already present, its pull is nearly impossible to ward off as a result of success's aftershocks.

Trying to match some internalized aesthetic ideal leads into one's head rather than simply surrendering to a process and working with the physical realities of one's own body. Self-censorship curtails freedom before expression is even begun.

Later, when we headed towards the Togo border, it was smooth sailing since the vice president's hometown region conspicuously lacked potholes and sported otherwise unseen streetlights and white safety lines. We passed the creepy "agricultural research center" with a hand-painted sign and towns swallowed whole by dams and res-ervoirs. A beauty salon oddly paid homage to Alabama, the state where so many ancestors went missing for centuries during the mass slavery era.

Guards at checkpoints eyed license plates and waved tourist cars like ours past hoping that we wouldn't witness the police extorting from the locals.

The villages nearer the border favor simple traditional structures. They are so likely to be burned down in recurring tribal land wars, that they don't bother with constructing more. There a 6 a.m. to 6 p.m. curfew is enforced, a government mandate making sure that people sleep. And *Okada* boy smugglers huddle on motocross-bikes near the border and wait.

We were made to wait under the afternoon sun outside an official witch camp. The former First Lady was due to arrive, buying votes with takeout lunches and handwaves. Predictably, her multivehicle entourage arrived hours late, and in the end the First Lady herself was a no-show and instead sent a representative—one of her sisters. This cavalcade of politician hypnotists—promise makers, promise breakers—quickly rushed on to the next stop.

Overall, the women were better off at the designated camps. They were forced there, though, to bow down and pray like nineteenth-century winos singing for their soup.

Throughout our travels, there was never any lack of those willing to share their experiences. But more than one woman was too overcome with emotion to continue.

A toddler wandered in during a tune and began to accompany on tin cans. A sound scientist, she was running experiments—conducting an exploration. The sympathy of her responses remain—evidence of synchronicity, the recording an acknowledgment of fate. Another song features a rubbed balloon, left over from the just-concluded rally.

As is often the case, when we thought we were done, we were really just getting started. Thus was spurred the journey hours onwards to the border and the search for villages where women were embedded furtively. The best song came last—fighting the loss of daylight and the obstructionism of the leaders who objected that she "wasn't a singer," I could see in her face that she was pregnant with expression. She stepped forth, opening a secret passageway within herself to deliver "You Left Me to Live Like an Animal," an opus lasting only minutes.

Over six hours of music was recorded with one hundred clandestines from across three villages. All but one sang solo for the first time. Nonetheless, in the end, indulged hipster bands from the West were easily outdone by a bunch of little old ladies with nothing to their name but voices.

Occasionally, men are also persecuted as witches, but they are deemed "wizards."

Feeling Left Out

One of the most undervalued abilities is to leave room in the music. A hyper-measuring society like ours overvalues action, rarely manifesting the maturity to *not* play anything, if it is not called for.

Consumerism trains us to accumulate. Digital recording lifted the previous limits of one-, two-, four-, eight-, sixteen-, twenty-four, and then forty-eight track analog recording. But the escalation of options has not produced better music. Just *more* of it.

Post-television America is arguably the least musical but most documented culture of all time. There reaches a point where excessive artifacts act as a substitute to creative action more than a source.

Ted Sommer was a drummer for Sinatra and many of Woody Allen's classic films. He exhibited a rare elasticity to bob and weave around a beat. I once sat, knees to his hi-hat—the only spot left in a fifty-seat club—and watched him lean back and spend an entire epic song with his arms crossed, reaching out only to accent three notes on a woodblock during the bridge. But sometimes it is one flourish that can make or break, tipping an entire song.

Witnessing countless soundchecks by other bands made clear: the bigger the kit, the worse the drummer.

One note should be worth a thousand words.

It is much like the use of negative space in visual arts, where every inch of a canvas need not be peppered and occupied. The greatest resonance can come from what is implied beyond the frame.

And so it is that silence can amplify.

Simple tends to be the hardest thing to do, for it requires faith. And restraint is devalued in any culture that worships excess.

In the West's musical system, most of the time for centuries we've sniffed around the possibilities of just seven of twelve notes. But even if a song is played loudly versus softly, it is no longer the same tune. It becomes as distinct as coffee served hot or iced. Blown through a toy sax, it is sundrenched. On cello, underwater and blurred. Notes can remain the "same" but transform.

Though many of my favorite albums of all time are composed of just one protracted piece (by Fela, Alvin Lucier, and Ornette Coleman, to name a few), as soon as possible, the music should stop. I have released a wide range—from songs that reach nearly twenty minutes to entire albums in which almost every track is less than a minute. Records should be only the length that is needed to deliver the most powerful message.

When Peter Lorre's unhinged character in the cinema classic *M* whistles one melody recurrently—often while unseen—the sound is made all the more unsettling since it is the only music in the entire almost two-hour film. (This was a rebound for director Fritz Lang: working with sound for the first time, he was no longer *required* to use music throughout the entire duration as he was forced to do with silent films where the noise from the projectors had to be masked from the audience.)

Great records should not be made on a scale of years, but seconds. Not through pushing but allowing—by letting the subconscious excavate alchemy from the depths.

Hanoi Masters:
Stereotypes in Stereo

While touring Australia, Master Quoc from the Hanoi Masters became very excited meeting the aboriginal people due to their didjeridoo. It turned out that he could play the instrument, also.

This fact spread rapidly, morphing into the belief that some version of the didjeridoo was a traditional Vietnamese instrument, as well. It was an idea concocted by overeager ethnomusicologists all too happy to connect the nonexistent dots.

The reality was far simpler.

Master Quoc was just another ponytail-sporting hippie that liked playing "foreign" instruments, not so unlike his baby-boomer peers in Marin County or other enclaves throughout the West.

Similarly, strangers often mistake my mother-in-law's astrology predictions as possessing ancient African origin. In fact, her infatuation came from watching far too much daytime Italian television.

Also somewhat reminiscent are Sardinian friends who christened their son Todd because they thought it was "exotic." This is not so far akin from folks in Iowa City tattooing Chinese characters onto their outer thighs without knowing their true meaning.

Vietnam grows some of the finest coffee in the world—chocolatey, without bitterness. But stereotypes—such as Asia being a place of teas—impose limits over which and how many arenas each culture is deemed worthy to excel in.

Immigrant communities tend to remain frozen in whatever era that they arrived. Italian-Americans warmth and joviality is more a reflection on late-nineteenth-century mores (as well as the precise microregions that most immigrants originated from) than jibing with modernized, northern Italy's stoicism.

Black Pride icon James Brown lifted his cape-draping resurrection stage bit from a "good ol' boy" peckerwood pro wrestler. Sources—conscious and unconscious—are complex and often accidental, and having been the first at something doesn't automatically equal being the best.

A common illusion is that culture is handed down as a throughline, seamless and unfractured. But much is formed using reconstructed memory aided-and-abetted by errors of omission, addition, or multiplication. Rather than tidy and linear, influence is more commonly an overlapping, concurrent, and/or elliptical, generation skipping feat.

In many ways, every place acts as such a Rorschach test. Each person tends to see what they want to see (or have been forced to). My childhood associations of Oakland feature Sonny Barger of the Hells Angels and Black Panther Huey Newton patrolling the streets with their respective posses. More than once, our family was enveloped along Interstate 580 by the thunder of a Hells Angel pack riding in formation. They'd surround us menacingly for a few miles—shouting back and forth over their engines—and then move on.

Decades later, I worked conducting triage interviews in the city's psychiatric emergency room, an experience that can make even the most milquetoast municipality seem downright dystopian.

The fingerprints have been wiped from the cultural origins of most things. Priests, griots, and rabbis were the true OGs, rapping over backing music since before Christ's time. And stained-glass cathedrals fashioned the first psychedelic lightshows. Through religion, multimedia was born.

All Hole, No Soul

Except for westernized artists, I've never once had a musician stop mid-performance and start over. To do so is evidence of being up in one's head, vigiling rather than relinquishing control.

One should never quit but play as if one's life depended on it. Birth labor cannot be halted midway, nor can a street fight.

The risk is that almost any time someone has a fallback plan, they end up falling back. It is an indulgence, a luxury. Instead, the integrity of each performance should be respected—a nonnegotiable oath.

Later, when reviewing any piece, it's best done with a macro view—holistically—rather than obsessing over any given "error." Micro details tend to get glossed over that instead can lend life to an arc and arrest a listener's attention. Those "little things" unveil a moment's truth.

20

Really "Real"?

Looked into your eyes.
Tried to see what was there.
But it seemed there wasn't room left
for anyone,
but you.

For me, "genuine" is determined by whether a communication springs more from the person's heart or head—more a cry than moan.

Sounds born from extraordinary events cannot be faked well—whether a belly laugh, orgasm, or cardiac arrest. Their very full-throatedness—even when stifled—remains ingrained if heard.

Here is a four-step authenticity diagnostic:
   a) Become alert whenever there is a marked shift between someone's speaking and singing voice. A mismatched tone—as if pasted on—is almost always a dead giveaway for fraud.
   b) Note whenever someone points while singing. The forefinger is at the forefront of presentationalism. These gestures more resemble junior staff members delivering a sales report at a weekly managerial meeting than artists.
   c) When faces are contorted frozenly—a pinched nose or cheeks—as if shitting out the music, without fail emotional constipation is present.

d) In contrast, when people sing with their entire person, their voices do not tire. They can go on almost endlessly as the sound originates from someplace else—without effort or force, it's simply allowed to happen.

The less truthful a performance, the more notes that get added—much like a liar who doesn't trust their story enough and is prone to blurting too much. I recently heard a star turn a single note into seven (!) with one of the most acute cases of *melisma* ever contracted—potentially even fatal. If not for him, then for the listener.

Generally, when vocalists allow themselves only one note per syllable, the performance is more mature.

In Havana I once attended an entire night of Tango by visiting Argentines. The acrobatics were jaw-dropping, but the entire stage was stolen by an aged and obese couple. They danced forehead to forehead, gliding and guiding each other without touching hands, as if hovering across a Ouija board.

When a performer concentrates and contains themself, the audience focuses, too, and the slightest gesture—a raised eyebrow or head nod rather than bombast—can send an entire arena into hysterics.

21

Naturally Higher

My daughter wrote her first song today.

Or, I should say, she improvised a recurring vocal melody while accompanying herself on guitar.

Nineteen months old and with just four notes, she bettered anything I've ever done. It might be the best thing she will ever do, as well.

I can only guard and pray that her expressiveness will not grow less pure and more censured over time.

It is not easy being two years old. Emotions pull you under like sleeper waves.

But even these too will pass.

Imperfection is a necessity for growth.

Learning to walk is learning to fall. Learning to run, never forgetting how to fly.

A Song Only a Mother Could Love

Just as my mother's ability to speak and feed herself waned, my daughter's speech burgeoned. She bloomed newly born, as an ocean away my own parent shriveled to nothingness.

It was after my mother hadn't spoken a word in months, that my father played one of my oldest and most misguided albums in the background. A nursing aide asked who it was. Unexpectedly, my mom struggled to reply.

"I-an," she said, without opening her eyes or further comment.

These were the last words she managed.

Music can potentially reach a "locked" brain stem. Even my music which was so second-rate it hadn't so much been forgotten, as never noticed.

It was a song that only a mother could love.

And it was the last link we shared, dovetailing with my daily attempts to reach past my daughter's preverbal cocoon via extemporaneous melodies and fingersnaps.

Often, I'd rest my head against her tiny chest and listen. It sounded like tomorrow.

IV.

LIBERATING SPIRIT THROUGH SOUND:

Choosing Life over Things

22

Like Cutters Trying
to Locate the Pain

People crave honesty. They receive so little of it in their everyday life that they can even become starved for it. Often greater intimacy and bonds have forged with a long-deceased artist, than anyone alive or that the listener has ever met.

Artists should model truth, for solace is sought in song.

Anyone who thinks that Taylor Swift is speaking to them authentically, needs a therapist.

And anybody who listens to Nina Simone, already has one: her.

Most modern singers operate on illusion. Their fans have never really heard them—no unbroken performance that is not airbrushed and punched-in; no live show without a guide track, if not entirely feigned. Like a partner who has not once seen their partner sans makeup—one who even sleeping naked, keeps eyeliner and blush on.

Rather than bringing a listener closer to the artist, too often layers of sound are used as emotional insulation, a sonic shield warding against true personal exposure—clinical, fully sanitized.

What we should seek is not perfect time but sympathetic response—someone who remains consistent to their own internal flow. What often makes a percussionist or dancer stand out—what constitutes their "style"—is the internal polyrhythms they bring to a pattern. They are doing the same movements as everyone else in a chorus line, but nonetheless feeling and expressing them differently. With the corrections made to most recordings now, these are the types of textures that are lost.

No matter how maligned, it is often cocktail acts that sing with the greatest pathos known. When forced to ride out empty or inattentive rooms, it is there that the last vestiges of self-consciousness are shed. Some of the most stellar performances ever staged have been cabaret covers that've fallen upon deaf ears—met with zilch applause, not even a half-handed charity clap.

23

Who Do You Love?

Spoken and written language can be translated informationally, but not contextually. Messages are interpretable to bi- or multilingual outsiders but not understood completely in their every nuance.

Similarly, Beethoven can never be heard the exact way it was written and intended, no matter how faithfully executed. Any ground-breaking work's very inception changes how people subsequently hear everything else and with each repetition this metamorphous continues, dulling the impact of original stimulus.

Rather than blends and complexity, presentationalists sing happy songs as if they are only happy. And sad songs as if only sad. What they've missed is that there's so much more to each line, as to almost all things.

Instead, they hold emotions hostage—not as transient experiences, but permanent states—and then try to wring them out, far in excess of their worth.

24

Sold Soul

"*Consume* music."

What an evil phrase.

It is a cancer, an idea so toxic that a HAZMAT team could be brought in.

Lip-synching is just bad pantomime—an edgier Marcel Marceau with backing track. In many cases it would be an improvement if such singers would fall mute entirely, like how watching an awful film with the sound off can often sharpen it or how it is oftentimes far scarier *not* seeing something and only having it indicated, instead.

They are the "Blue-eyed soul"-*less* singers, witlessly advancing a white supremacist agenda.

The peddled goods are impersonations of copies *of copies*. They trade in clones—remakes of songs that would've better never been made in the first place.

The Good Ones carry on the music passed down to them by Janvier's blind brother, who perished in the genocide.

The Good Ones (Rwanda): I Love You Even If You Break My Heart

Because the Good Ones' first two albums attracted the admiration of one the world's most famous "roots" groups, a London charity offered the Rwandan band a gourmet organic dinner in London headed by a celebrity chef. The organizers were convinced that detail would prove the clincher in getting the group to agree to perform for free at an annual benefit fundraiser for Africa.

More than anything, what the promoters had missed was that the band were all itinerant farmers from Africa who themselves were well in need and possessed no means—monetary or visa-wise—to hop on a long-distance, two-day international flight at will. Not to mention that *everything* the musicians ate was already organic. So much so, that they were stumped what the term "organic" could even mean, as they'd never considered that food existed otherwise.

We recorded the Good Ones' third album at their leader Adrien's hillside farm—the one that he and his children were born on, the place where he'd hid for months in the trees nearby to survive the genocide.

The Good Ones manage without electricity and running water, luxuries that have yet to reached their remote region despite the nation's advancement. And even if these utilities ever make it there physically, they might still remain beyond the band members' reach financially.

Looking down into Adrien's wide and askew valley—one that is folded and hidden within other valleys beyond the paved roads—the lush and multihued forest is dizzying.

I do not wallow in despair, fetishizing suffering. Nor do I trade in poverty porn or tragedy.

I am not seeking primitivism, but minimalism. The value of spareness.

Starvation is not a gimmick. It is a reality. And individuals facing such challenges should not be denied a stage for discourse, tolerated only if they conform to superimposed Anglo standards of style, affect, and instrumentation.

We have played the Good Ones' music for scads of expat Rwandans, and every response has been the same: "you can't find music like this anymore."

I've never heard a genocide survivor speak of strength. Only necessity.

Most artists in the West wane with age due to excess—drugs, ego, the objectification of others. But artists from less mechanized lands usually decline due to the opposite: *lack*. Of nutrition, healthcare, and adequate shelter.

Adrien's is a voice not deliberately rasped through blunts and tequila shots, but life itself. As we parted, he handed me a sack of iron beans from his farm. Seeing the longing in his children's eyes as they watched this transaction, my urge was to refuse. But it was clear that he was seeking nourishment other than food and that acceptance of this generosity was nonnegotiable.

Every Task Inflates to Whatever Time Allowed

The Beatles' first full-length release was recorded in just over twelve hours.

And James Brown put out seven albums in 1970–1971 along with another five in 1969!

Rudy Van Gelder, the jazz great, recorded thousands of recordings in his parents' living room while still employed during the day as an optometrist. He later built a studio with deliberately high ceilings (anathema to standard studio methodology), and it was there that *A Love Supreme* was recorded—in just one session.

For less than the sum that so many ho-hum bands squander on a single day in the studio tweaking a snare sound (one that they are likely to scrap later anyway, only to start anew), entire records from neglected artists and regions around the world could be leased life.

Mulligo from the Malawi Mouse men pounds out customized beats on his found-percussion kit.

Malawi Mouse Boys: Getting Down and Dirtier

Monstrous power lines fly over the Malawi Mouse Boys homes without ever touching down. Yet, the band continues to live without electricity, receiving all of its radiation but none of the perks.

Just because some diplomat's kid skateboards in a capital's downtown doesn't change the fact that the majority of a population live on starvation's edge. It's the worst kind of cosmetic trickery—like an insipid pop singer sporting a mohawk and carving "renegade" in their arm.

Same as almost everywhere in the world, out by the Mouse men's village, the divisions are vast between urban and rural worlds. People pass on dirt roads, literally by the truckload—on their way to anywhere, but here.

A journalist visiting from the city set his iPad on the band's animal-skin tom drum, using it as a desk after squatting uninvited on their throne. It is nearly impossible to imagine an equivalent demonstration of disrespect happening elsewhere—a *Rolling Stone* reporter putting his feet up on one of Metallica's amps? He'd be shitcanned by security in minutes.

This display was followed by the indelicate and repulsed refusal of their fellow countrymen to taste mice when offered by the band. Worse, they cringed watching the men swallow the refused delicacy whole—head, tail, and all—much the same way many eat sardines.

Suffice to say that almost no one goes Gluten-free among their neighbors. Nor are strawberry or peanut allergies found.

During WWII, peasant families in war-torn Europe would slather lard on bread to load up on absent calories. Today, the rich malnourish themselves on purpose.

I think back to my wife's father's tales of eating rats and cats during Italy's postwar devastation. By the time he was in his twenties, the nation was abuzz with Vespas and televisions. The story lends some hope how quickly change can come, both for better and worse.

Despite their good fortune in performing overseas, the Malawi Mouse members continue to teeter on the edge of famine.

They are not underprivileged, but *un*privileged by most measures.

When we were lucky enough to visit the USA with the group, they saluted the Empire State Building with a shrug, perplexed that I was signaling out just one building after the deluge of skyline that they'd been marveling at during the past hour's ride from JFK Airport.

When they'd first arrived in the USA, their entry was delayed hours beyond normal. A seasoned officer at San Francisco Airport said it was the first Malawian passport he'd ever seen in his decades-long career. His guess was that the country was located somewhere in Asia.

It was probably I, the driver that was most startled during a long ride by the group's panic as we approached a truncated tunnel. It was a constriction that they'd never encountered before—since there are not tunnels yet in their entire nation. They described it as "going in the pot," to be boiled alive.

As we sat at a twenty-four-hour trucker café along Interstate 5, a high-school-age server grew impatient with the band's celebratory nature at the experience of being waited on in a restaurant. It was then that she nuked me via an elongated, forceful blink beneath her tattooed, two-shades-too-light brow. She failed at casting the spell to make us all disappear from her midst forever but succeeded quite handily in dampening their joy.

Worse may've been the taxi driver that refused their fare for fear he'd contract Ebola, a disease that had reached America but never Malawi.

Seeing their stunned and unabashed reaction to a woman walking two poofy and ribboned toy poodles through an airport terminal was the yin-yang of the bone-through-the-nose cannibal stereotype.

Hearing "Hotel California," queasy on a tape deck at the end of a dead-end, Malawian lake dirt-road spoke eloquently for itself as metaphor. The residents didn't know who sang it. For them, it was just tourist bait.

On that same mountain road, the severity of endemic anger lead a shirtless boy a football field away to heave a cinder block at the first white face he saw—me. The projectile futilely fell, just missing his toes. He'd sent murderous rage towards a car otherwise full of locals. Nonetheless, he was that much in need of some place for his feeling to land. So much better, if it had been through song.

The last time I visited Mulligo's home, we blew a tire due to tree stump remnants encroaching on the path's last stretch. Within less than an hour, some neighborhood kids were able—without the help of a jack—to fix the flat. Alas, on the way back out, we ended up stuck in the drainage ditch, incapable of traversing its depth.

Success is perilous as it can't help but change people. In most cases not right away, but gradually. With the Mouse Men, Mulligo bought a bike, but soon wrecked it, breaking out his front teeth—a concrete example of watching out for what "good fortune" might set in motion.

The Mouse Men wait their turn and endure. Placeholders for some future generation, they exude the irrecoverable exhaustion of those unable to let their guard down for far too long, if ever.

25

Unmasking Precedents

Spitting with each word, he insisted, "But what they are doing *is* from a tradition of masking. I've studied it." He became so pinkish, his cheeks about burst from fury. His man-bun came partially undone, falling about his shoulders.

The issue in question was the Malawi Mouse Boys donning a Halloween mask mid-set for one song.

Little did this ethnomusicologist in New Zealand realize that it was all a ruse that had nothing to with any ancient heritage but had been my own stupid idea—a whim that the band agreed to try once for kicks to see how it played with the audience (and which, in fact, ended up falling quite flat).

My sheepish confession was not enough for him, though.

"No! They're drawing from the southern African vocal tradition. The same one as Ladysmith Black Mambazo and the other groups that have influenced them."

Try as I might, I could not impress upon him that not only had the band never heard of Ladysmith Black Mambazo, they had no idea who Paul Simon was either.

And on a continent of a billion-plus people, why should they?

Just because the West christens someone, it doesn't necessarily hold any weight at home. Especially if it's been declared by an interloping individual who themselves is unknown and of little consequence amid such pockets of anonymity in their "worldwide" fame.

26

(mis-)reading minds

There are often two sides working in tandem to damage an accurate assessment of art:

On the one hand, there is the assumption of shared influence between like sounding artists.

On the other is the disregard for how commonly parallel invention occurs—great ideas that percolate from so deep down, they ultimately reach more than one outlet.

A prize-winning journalist was incessant in her non-acceptance that a Zomba prisoner had no knowledge of Johnny Cash.

She tried various angles of attack with him.

"You know, the guy with the deep voice?"

Then later, "The man all in black?"

She even attempted a bad baritone impersonation, as if that could rewrite cultural divides and bring "the undertaker" back into being.

Similarly, a reviewer jabbered that the Malawi Mouse Boys had been inspired by "Mento" music. This despite the fact that the number of people anywhere who are familiar with Mento is beyond limited. It's absurd to then propose that among those select few would happen to be the Mouse men, who live without electricity and have listened to very little recorded music from anywhere—let alone pre-Ska and pre-Reggae Jamaican music from across the ocean. Obviously, this writer had just learned of the genre himself and couldn't wait to name-drop it at the first available chance.

For those who remain distant from mass media, whatever content they do receive likely arrives filtered. If ever they even hear a Beatles song, it is likely a reinterpretation (or even bastardization) by someone who probably hasn't the faintest who John Lennon is either.

27

Hazards of Hypercognition

The power of pop music was not that it is popular, but that it was *populist*.

Music is sacred because it transcends all religion, race, gender, age, and politics. It can potentially reach any one—crossing the largest physical distances this planet offers and touching the most disenfranchised. Generations can even be bridged and the dead speak to the living (or the barely living, in many cases).

Artists become stand-ins, rough drafts of God.

But this depersonalization—the dislocation of soundwaves from their source—can also lead to music's misuse. How many priests have molested altar boys to sacred Gregorian chant soundtracks? How many love songs have been debased to sell hemorrhoid medication, petroleum, and nicotine gum?

Move someone's heart (or ass) and the mind will follow. The trick is to change their brain when they're not looking—while pleasantly distracted—in much the same way that the jester is the only one usually allowed to speak the truth to the king.

In Puglia, I watched two strangers at a restaurant—a racist northerner and a "*terroni*" from the south—without making eye-contact, spontaneously sing to each other, off-key from across the divide. Decades down—for the space of a song—some national classic retained the power to unite divisions that otherwise remained unbridged.

28

Commercialization Choking on Its Own Waste

Corporations are word thieves.

By commercializing communication, it is boxed-in, and oxygen is siphoned from the collective imagination, emptying symbols of meaning.

Just a few of the songs that have ripped words right out of people's mouths:

Beat It
What's Going On?
Summertime
Walk This Way
Crazy
Don't Worry (Be Happy)
Satisfaction (I Can't Get No)
New York, New York

Good luck trying to speak any of these words and phrases without having them sung back to you sarcastically in response.

And, have mercy on any one whose name has been memorialized in a pop song—"Daniel," "Mary, Mary," or "Hey, Joe." To daily have your own name turned satire by mere acquaintances has to be one of life's great indignities.

My own brother may have had it the worst. He was christened with the rarity Jude. Five years *later* that moniker became a Beatles hit and led forevermore to most everyone assuming that he'd been named after a song that did not yet exist and in tribute to a group that my parents had never heard of and, in the end, were never fans of.

Sometimes linguistic turf can be reclaimed through slang or irony, but most often it must be forfeited entirely. Whoever is the most famous bullies and gains ownership of a term. There are many San Franciscos, but only one gets to be *the* "San Francisco." And heaven forbid that a serial killer seizes your identity—leaving you to live out the remainder of your days trailed by a legacy that is not your own.

Mass media wears words down to nubs.

29

Dysfunction Junction: Repeating Something Over and Over Again, Still Doesn't Make It True

An over-cited story about John Cage was his startle at hearing his own circulatory system after he'd entered an anechoic chamber. This has since repeatedly served as purported proof that there is no real "silence."

But the sad fact is that medically, the average person cannot hear one's own system—even in such a chamber—unless something's malfunctioning with their cardiac health. Therefore, Mr. Cage's sensation might more have been a missed opportunity to diagnose early the arteriosclerosis that over time contributed to his death.

Unfortunately, neat narratives prevail in most arm-wrestles with truth.

Various peers of Woody Guthrie noted young Zimmerman's bizarre transformation after meeting the "Dust Bowl Troubadour" who by that time was interned to an infirmary. Dylan's trademark mannerisms while playing—the odd head tics and mouth contortions—seemed a sublimated forgery of Guthrie's own Parkinsonian symptoms. Dylan had never known the pre–Parkinson's disease, robust freight-hopping, and picket-line-manning Guthrie.

Pop culture's very pathways quite possibly were inadvertently infected and colonized, not by artistic vision, but the physical malady of his idol.

The Bee Gees managed to become one of the biggest-selling groups of all-time in part by trying midcareer to sound like black singers and failing, but crashing ass-backwards into a distinctive style due to their thick Aussie accents.

By way of failed cultural transmission, on the display card of a Neapolitan bar jukebox we stumbled into one morning, Grand Funk Railroad becomes *Brand* Funk Rail *Dad*—a much better name, by the way.

A lion's share of last names throughout the world are misspellings, accidents manifested by illiterate ancestors.

This is our true heritage—one riddled with error.

Squeezing Out a Spark

It was there in an overgrown California cul-de-sac, strewn with stripped muscle cars, outboard motor boats, and other dreams deferred and put up on blocks: a tract home caught between the awkward phase of no longer being brand spanking new, but not yet acquiring the vintage and quaint status it would eventually accrue by accident. This was where a treasure trove of pop culture lay hid, in the form of scattered and moldy LP jackets, strewn across two adolescent brothers' room and sharing real estate on the textile carpet beside skidmarked, white jockey underpants dropped inside out, lying for weeks where disrobed.

When people ask where I am from, I'm tempted to answer, "Some place that no longer exists."

The energy of places is unstable, altered by time. The same buildings can withstand socioeconomic forces that reshuffle around them. Gentrification moves communities wholesale beyond city centers, forming ever-further, concentric circles of exclusion.

For many latchkey kids that were left partial refugees amid the 1970s divorce explosion, mass media acted as surrogate father.

In that era, each album, every song was a gamble. With contents locked in shrink-wrap, we could only go on hunches and hearsay. Actual discovery of what lay inside required the commitment of dollars to the cause—money made with predawn paper routes and babysitting jobs where the mothers paid in whatever crumpled singles and quarters they dredged from the bottom of their purses.

The brothers opened a world to me—Girlschool, Leonard Cohen, the Smiths, Angel City, Jonathan Richman. It did not matter that some of these artists would prove not the mightiest the world had to offer.

What mattered was that they offered at least some substance, voices reaching out from the void, signals received across continents and seas.

In borrowed cars, with the windows down we'd cross the Bay Bridge, the coffee roastery's metallic-mold scent hitting us before the skyscraper skyline had come fully in view. We used to chase the setting sun, right out to the Richmond's edge, where the Russian, Vietnamese, and Irish immigrants slammed up against the end of America. But we lost every time. Stranded beside Sutro Baths' remains, there was nowhere further to run. We were left to scream into the surf, songs we only pretended to know.

A perfect prescription for art is not needed. Regardless, it effects a biochemical action, dredging something that lay dormant inside us.

And for that I owe my long-lost friends. For most people's lives often hinge not on sudden revelation or a vivid instant, but on some tiny pivot that shifts their focus and leads the way out from where and to what class they were born—modern-day cloaked caste systems.

Scarcity creates concentration and a potency that often overcomes quantity. When you are starving, scraps become a meal—other people's waste, your feast. And one song or image can carry. What's extrapolated is some core power, partially crystallizing a culture. One makes the most of whatever clues can be found and tries to back-engineer based on those assumptions—much like crushing inward on an atom and hoping for implosion. Culture is the collective affect of a people, the resting-face baseline. It is not that anyone is without influence. It is just that in mass media's absence, influence comes from fewer elements—sometimes mapped from the DNA of a single song.

Not everyone necessarily need read *Hamlet*, but they need to read *something*. They aren't required to watch *Mean Streets* or *I Vitelloni*, but they do need stories—*any* story.

For the difference between nothing and something is not simple arithmetic—one is not merely one more than zero but incalculably greater.

It taps infinity.

La Gomera:
The Canary Island Whistlers

To sit at a beach café overlooking the last harbor Christopher Columbus docked his three ships before heading out and invading America can't help but inspire a shitstorm of what-ifs.

La Gomera is a small island off the coast of northwest Africa, a place where the ancient whistling language, *Silbo*, is still used. It is a system that arose for farmers to communicate across fields. To keep it from dying, the government now mandates that it be taught in schools. But, sadly, it's mostly voiced today as amusement of the day-tripper busloads of retirees that flock in-and-out for the experience.

It is an island that you that you can circle in mere hours, but is folded into so many rocky, brain-like crevasses, that if it were spread flat the circumference would inflate to proper nation-size. The wind there is at a constant taut, rendering the noise floor quite deafening as if it were a call beckoning one to be carried away on the tides rather than remain there for long. And carved into the steeply rising coastline's side is a wide, suspiciously nuclear silo looking tunnel.

The Buena Vista Social Club's sounds have rebounded back here, infiltrating the local rhythms and phrasing, as wine-soaked pensioners who use their chins like exclamation points while away their days in an upstairs bar. Oblivious on the block below, preteens attempt to stave off the passing of summer by stubbornly sporting short-shorts weeks after the chill has set in. Flair there is displayed by designer loafers, not hot rods.

Instead of dancers mirroring live music and feeding back cross-rhythms for musicians to mimic, today an arena-concert cliché is shouting, "Turn the lights up so I can see you." It raises the question,

"Just who have they been performing for this entire time?" Literally those they can't see or even know for certain are there.

Many claim that the Blues in America was not born until after slavery, when the resulting displacement and isolation forced accompanying oneself rather than being accompanied—a death knell for collaborative music-making.

The West's binary tendencies split most instruments into right and left—the passive side handling rhythm and the dominant, leading melodically. It is a defiance of most traditions where music is realized with greater balance—ambidextrous and evenhanded.

Relatedly, when virtuosity is made king musically, competition rather than communion are engendered.

Once, in Ghana we witnessed a family of five play the equivalent of a trap kit, but with each age group responsible for just one of its pieces. They'd restored the instrument to its source, as it was before collectivity imploded in the early days of the Industrial Age and drum-corps shrunk to piecemeal, one-person affairs. Prior to that, it took an entire village to rock.

On the stairs, the aged but youngest member of the drunken lot shook my hand as strongly as he was able. It was far in excess of a salutation, as if it were not already evident how much his grip dwarfed mine. He drilled down into my eyes and insisted, "I am a *professional*." It was then that he revealed himself, much more graphically than he ever could've intentionally hoped to. Favoring one side, his smile gnarled, more lie than truth.

It is better to not profess how long you've done something, but how well. A lot of people suck at their jobs, sometimes for an entire career.

If someone grows defensive and challenges, "Do you know how many records/films/etc. I've worked on?" the answer is easy.

"*Too* many."

Whether one or innumerable, every project is best treated as the first and last, a matter of life and death.

For all we know, it might very well be.

Accidental Implosion

The trio set up on the asphalt of my elementary school's basketball court, the one featuring frayed steel-mesh nets. Since there was no PA, the band were forced to plug their vocal mic into an SVT bass rig.

It was the Loopty Lu fundraiser and the opening act had been the accordion duo of my German-immigrant neighbor, a middle-aged man with indelibly beet-red skin and India-ink-soaked hair. He'd booked the band solely based on the twelve-year-old drummer being the son of a friend who attended the same evangelical church—nepotism is rarely without a home.

Little did the elder know the fury was about to be unleashed upon his suburban circle.

This was a year after the Sex Pistols stormed out of London—when Sid Vicious was still among the living and the band had yet to plough into the quicksand of San Francisco for their final concert (the site of the Beatles' last performance, as well).

They wore thrift store, tweed jackets and skinny ties, consequently, roasting in the direct, high-noon sun. They seemed on their way somewhere—sailing fast—even while standing still. With catawampus hair that defied gravity, their din literally incited families to disperse and run. More people than not—from toddlers to elderly—plugged their ears reflexively, using both index fingers. Women with wigs screamed back at the singers' screaming, mounting inaudible attempts to get the group to turn down.

The songs were one-minute (or less) blasts of energy, every single word indecipherable.

And I'd fallen under the spell.

This marks the exact point where musicologists generally fail when theorizing about context. Context *does* matter, but it is a moving target and differs for each individual.

A local garage band from a town most people have never heard of, who only played one "show" ever, and whose name I never even knew, had more impact on me than most "content" of my generation.

And it was not due to the quality of anything that they did, but what it pointed towards.

30

Letting Go

The world is not "my oyster."

It is not mine at all.

It belongs to someone else. Maybe, if we are lucky, for a moment it becomes ours on loan.

But from the first breath, we're being ushered towards the door.

A map to the messiah, a shot at redemption, art can prepare us for death—to surrender ego and embrace our own finiteness.

A guide to continuously live as if death is imminent, as if there are no guarantees. In other words: to live as things actually are.

The quest is not a search for exoticness or to travel as remotely as possible, but to hear more carefully. Tony Schwartz—arguably the best field recordist ever—was agoraphobic, lived with his mother, and never recorded more than twenty blocks from his home. Luckily for him, he lived in densely populated, diverse Manhattan. There he documented the life of his dog, taxi horns, and neighborhood playground games, among others.

The solution is not making the world our smorgasbord, ramping up the arms race of consumption. Better to listen to Nina Simone unravel "Just Like Tom Thumb's Blues" or Sandy Denny sing "Who Knows Where the Time Goes?" a hundred times than rush to snap shots at every prescribed hotspot such as the Grand Canyon and Eiffel Tower.

What legacy do I wish to leave behind?

I don't.

If any, invisibility.

I hope (and *expect*) to be forgotten. I eventually will be anyway.

Music bends the air and through that process can reshape the soul.

V.

RAISING OUR VOICES:

Singing Back the Tidal Wave

31

Tyrannical Tech:
Social Media Suckled Suckers
Stalking Themselves

Hordes now hold their screens up like shields, almost unable to walk without a device leading the way.

Feeding frenziedly on endless feedback loops of self, they place their faith in the latest handheld salvation.

But we already have a technology that can save us: music.

It has before. Many times over.

In art, emotion should come before precision. And in life, emotion is better given its due as a counterbalance to intellect.

As recording advanced, geeks were increasingly entrusted power over the artistic process. These were technicians who not infrequently had only a passing interest in music, often tended towards reclusive and even antisocial conduct, and profited personally from the recording procedure itself becoming elongated. Nonetheless, they became the first listeners, influencing or even guiding outcomes.

Ironically, one of the biggest changes that interferes with capturing sound in high-fidelity is technology itself. Ever-present cellphone signals now wreak havoc with files encoding properly. It is not the devices ringing unexpectedly as much as their being nearby and powered on. If discovered after the fact, the random squiggly intrusions phones cause are irreparable.

It is better to do something "dumb" smartly (think Bon Scott or Mo'Nique) than to hide behind the cerebral, unartfully executed.

The roots of the word "media" itself remain revealing. A medium is a person who claims the ability to contact and speak to people who are dead, and to pass messages between them and the people still alive. But "medium" can also mean mediocre.

We don't so much need plastic-surgery-honed, proxy Gods or American witch doctor pharmaceutical giants. We require stronger depth of communication between individuals.

The original backup of data is conversing, transferring memory to each other.

Hearing is memory—becoming conscious of something that has already occurred. Through the instant nostalgia of a song's hook, we surf the edge of disappearance.

Recording is a shadow captured and made corporeal. Since the dawn of time, people were terrified by disembodied sound.

Today, we've come to seek comfort in it.

Counterfeit Prophets: Using Technology as a Crutch

One of the most important things an artist can do?
NOTHING!!!

Our cognitive-overkill, device-dependent society tends towards a preoccupation with being occupied. Lost (or at least massively misplaced) is summoning the courage to face and embrace monotony—to practice patience and just sit still.

Listen to your own footsteps (to show where you are headed). Try to hear the "quiet."

The brain and spirit must be allowed leisure. Boredom is not a state to be feared but *revered* as a trigger. Most of us find our way by getting lost, through a series of dead ends.

Don't tune technique. Soften your heart.

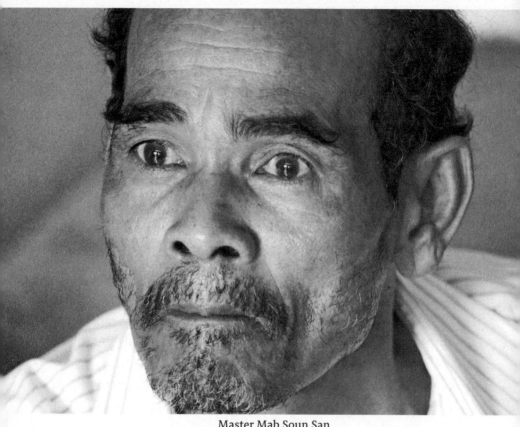

Master Mab Soun San
(Khmer Rouge Survivors)
1950–2017

Khmer Rouge Survivor: the unnoticed passing of a master

Master Mab Soun San lived a few hundred yards from the edge of Phnom Penh airport's landing strip where the planes would buzz and almost clip his building's rain gutters. It was there that he endured the unhampered tirade of rich foreigners' often whimsical arrivals and departures—invasions and occupations. He instead remained stuck and immobile in the land that had once marked him for murder.

A few months earlier, at age sixty-six, he had just gotten his first passport. He was set to leave on his maiden voyage, in order to perform in the UK. He said it was his dream. But before it could happen, he slipped twice into coma and then was gone.

A supremely gifted singer vanished without fanfare, escaping the notice of all but his family. Such is the fate of most artists. And it is the listeners' loss, ultimately.

He had been burdened with a permanent limp from the days during the genocide. In his final months he descended into a wheelchair, then slumped entirely horizontal, bedridden. That is how he then remained until the end.

Though he'd struggled to cross his tiny one-room apartment, when he played, all calamities lifted and this man who could barely walk seemed to fly, almost levitating. For a spiritual experience, in lieu of the Angkor Wat shrine, pilgrims would have been well-advised to visit Soun San instead.

Once, he sang as if in a trance until the song neared the thirteen-minute mark. Seated beside him on a mattress without a frame his wife had been sewing stoically, but suddenly rose and shook him by the shoulders, bringing him back down from wherever his spirit had traveled. I have often wondered how long he would have gone on had she not felt the need to intervene. I like to believe he'd still be playing now, that the song would have sustained him.

His body failed, but the music never left him. And in some parallel, more just universe his voice lives on.

32

Hungering for Connection: Sloppy Kisses, at Best

Knowingly or not most people love mistakes—for asymmetry is fundamental to beauty.

The majority of favorite performance stories I've ever heard are about when something went off the rails during a show—the time the singer unintentionally flashed his penis or the power went out or the band had to stop and restart a song three times. The larger allure these provide is that everyone present survived and lived to tell about it, having shared an unrepeatable moment. This is the same reason that parents relish recounting near-miss stories about their children's travesties *after the fact*—it is proof of grace. Ultimately, these instances are about recovery and redemption, and we are nothing if not a salvation-story-jonesing nation.

Concerts at their best are a form of mass group-therapy, inspirational rather than anesthetizing—not a means to deny but to confront and purge pain.

From Russia with Love (and Ambivalence)

Walking through East Berlin following the aftermath of the wall coming down, I once dodged a drunk and shirtless man as he stomped through an underground pedestrian tunnel. Clasping a WWII-issue pistol in his hand at waist level, he held it not menacingly, but unhurried and matter-of-factly. This made it all the more unnerving.

In Moscow today, the whole city—even the trees—remain poker-faced. Long abandoned overpass columns stand half-built, rusted rebar sprouting willy-nilly from up top like a fuck you to no one in particular and everyone at the same time.

With a conspicuously all-female border agent force, it felt more like entering a Russ Meyer exploitation film than crossing the Iron Curtain. Garrisoned off inside themselves following Communist rule, the faces are stoic, but the graffiti looks the South Bronx same. Funk-guitar upbeats punctuate syrupy pop songs as if collusion of some sort instead occurred with Niles Rodgers illegitimate heirs.

The electronic duo I'd ventured there to meet, live along the city's far reaches in a nineteenth-century czar-era cabin set down pedestrian dirt paths with tall Tolstoy trees that outlasted both the Nazis and the Communist Party. Residents have to wade chest deep in snow during winter to reach their own door from the main road. As we walked along the river and past the statute commemorating the first two cosmonaut dogs in space, the group claimed that I was the first foreigner to have visited their neighborhood. Ever.

A world away downtown betwixt a sea of backwards "N's" and "R's," tourists snap pictures with Stalin lookalikes, his past somehow cleansed in a way Hitler's never could be while workers sleep off late-morning benders atop railway switch boxes dotting the tracks.

Former-KGB gangster pop stars flood the airwaves with French chanteuse-inspired music featuring ultraviolent prison lyrics that beg for mob leaders to bless them with "tattoos" and praising Jesus. It is Russia's version of "Country" music and can fill stadiums with potbellied, middle-aged men and their mistresses.

We recorded in a hobo encampment beneath the train-track bridge. Later we trespassed inside a former Soviet factory complex that took up entire blocks of prime waterfront. The sputter and spew of a duct-taped ventilator accompanied us, and the rust streaks below the aluminum-framed windows above looked like each floor had wept toxins.

There was a time not so long ago that Russian citizens could be jailed for listening to American music. Following the end of Communist rule, there was an initial rush of hearing English-language artists. Gradually, though, the novelty has dimmed and citizens have turned back to local stars instead.

History Does Not Repeat, It Merely Morphs and Searches for a Fresh Host

My dad couldn't teach me what I wanted to learn, so he taught what he knew, instead: that life was hard.

He willfully ignored how time itself would teach us that fact, many times over. He forced us to mow lawns midday, steeping in the former farmland heat while using a machine with no muffler and minus the sack that catches the grass. Our work was more than doubled by the subsequent raking and bagging this required. All this was aside from the machine possessing a cracked crank-and-pull starter that sometimes would take an hour of attempts to ignite.

More than a sadistic act, we were raised—like many/most—under the specter of unresolved hurt. My father's own mother died suddenly when he was eight. We were consequently reared amid the constant threat from our own mother's precarious health.

By chance, decades later I ended up regularly lecturing on conflict resolution at the same psychiatric ward where she'd been detained. I'd come full circle, institutionalized from the other side. It was a locked unit and children were not allowed inside. On Christmas Eve, from the second-floor window she'd waved to me on the sidewalk below, her face pressed against the glass.

As part of her recuperation, my dad bought my mother a used upright. She'd played as a child and the doctors thought it would help her healing. She rarely touched it, but when she did it was only if unwitnessed. I could hear her hesitantly peck out the notes as if sending messages in code. All other activity in the house would cease, suspended as we probed for meaning that she could not otherwise share.

Often, the most stirring sound was the attack and decay of her closing the piano's fallboard, only to withdraw once again.

33

As the Heart Grows, the Ego Shrinks, Making Room

Much of the best music occurs outside commerce, largely due to that person not seeking external validation through it. Instead, they play only for its own intrinsic value.

This is much the same reason why people are so attracted to antisocial performers. The inbred contradiction with that stance though is that why would anyone step onstage year after year if they didn't deeply care about and crave attention?

The thrust of punk rock was not that anyone could be a star. It was that there should be *no* stars at all.

Most don't want heroes anymore, though. They want someone like themselves that they can then worship. By celebrating another's ordinariness, they celebrate themselves.

Meanwhile, the majority of contributions and inspirations in life go uncredited—the workers that died to build a bridge that we cross twice daily, a person walking past who triggers an idea or reverie, a snippet of a song misheard and never identified but remembered in fragments forever.

Taking a wage job is not the worst thing that can happen to an artist. Particularly considering that almost the entire canon of folk music was written by laborers—farmers, fishermen, barbers, and slaves.

A media that encourages individualism and competition versus communalism discourages people from organizing and uniting for their own common good. This is the Stockholm syndrome of capitalism—many of those who suffer most under a system become its most ardent defenders.

If all things are put on the market, then so are we, and every breathing moment is reduced to performance.

With cutthroat commercialism, it is charity that's subjected to the highest scrutiny and suspicion. To dare accept selfless motives as pure possesses the power to upend profit's gangrene soul.

34

Voluntary Enslavement

As corporations merge, they no longer need so much to promote any particular product. All profits are increasingly channeled to the chosen few by way of their various brands merely acting as fronts and decoys—manufacturing the illusion of choice.

Instead, it is now consumerism as a lifestyle more than any specific item that is advertised.

And all for the greater un-good.

In a society that worships money, is it any wonder that billionaires become default deities?

Many now desperately amass products in much the same way our ancestors collected good luck charms—insurance against supernatural powers, a denial of death.

The internet trades in a form of gossip which has become more credible than the real world. It is the opposite of traditional Mafia—based not on who you know but on people you do *not* know.

And so, anonymous strangers wield their social media accounts like holstered guns and bystanders now more often record a fistfight than stop it.

Other people are used as currency, traded like cards.

Homogenous music transfers even greater power to corporations. They are no longer dependent on any individual artist, if they've become more or less interchangeable.

Don't Tell Me What You Think, Show What You Feel

Belaboring art does it a disservice. Creativity need not necessarily be an overtly painful operation. Good things can come from simply trusting yourself to express things truthfully and not getting tripped up worrying about results that match preexisting concepts. By getting out of our heads and surrendering to intuit inspiration, the spirit can be emancipated.

Performers will often complain, "I don't think I was good tonight." But music originates the heart, not the head.

Nonetheless, just because something feels good, doesn't mean it *is* good. Hindsight can provide surprising perspectives. After the prism of the present is lifted—some songs rise, while the "cream of the crop" have dissolved.

Almost everyone involved with a record believes that they are working on *Pet Sounds* or *Kind of Blue*, that a potential masterpiece is in the making.

They aspire to *Citizen Kane* but end up with *Citizen Shame*.

"Sure things" almost never are. And absolutes are for cowards.

But there is one sure thing that works all the time: accepting that certainty doesn't exist.

An important mantra is, "I don't know." Say it often.

Music should not be made for the fans of an artist, but for people who are otherwise indifferent or, even better, hate that person's work. Strive to create mind-changing music. This process can only occur away from the "yes people" and cheerleaders. I do not allow anyone to "hang out" during a recording, only those directly taking part.

As not all good things require suffering, contrastingly not all suffering is an indication that something is of worth (e.g., an addictive "love"). In general, if the experience becomes escalatingly painful, it's time to abandon that path—or at least take a temporary reprieve—and pursue a new approach.

It is advisable to not just always have a backup plan, but *plans*.

There is a world of difference between creative overdubbing—the threading of tapestries—versus endless, sonic-sanitizing punch-ins and redos.

The standout track on an album is usually the one that was done with ease *or* contrastingly the most overcooked. It is the middle that tends towards the most mediocre. If you're going to start down a road, you'd better come braced to go all the way ... and beyond. Otherwise, we end up in some no-man's-land—neither here nor there. And the way is almost always further than foreseen.

Ironically, what someone excels at will almost always remain a stepchild, neglected, almost resented for its existence.

It's moments that matter, more than consistent but tame takes. Modern mixes increasingly are so compressed that when heard from a distance and with any kind of background noise, almost no definition—not even the basic melody—can be discerned. They are ear-splittingly louder than classic heavy metal, but nonetheless flaccid.

Perfection is the enemy of progress. Momentum takes on a life of its own. Inertia is the state where most people remain stunted, never once ever really getting started. Instead, they perpetually remain delusional about what they can or will do (or *could've* done), rather than simply doing it. Most good intentions and grand ambitions are never freed from this morass. They die in the graveyard of each individual mind.

Fuzz tone itself was invented by accident. Not by the metalheads for whom it became indispensable, but by Country-Western engineering legend Glenn Snoddy.

As the sonics proliferate—and our actual surroundings are displaced by "surround sound"—the content has grown more monolithic.

Options in excess turn oppressive.

fra fra specialize in "funeral songs," but often the procession appears more a celebration.

fra fra:
Funeral Songs

Never trust a guy in a Santa hat. The economy-class race war broke out over a seat being leaned back too far and wasn't helped any by the all-white steward staff.

After disembarking, the regional airline took us onwards to the predominantly Muslim northern region. Their in-flight magazine featured "retail therapy" propaganda and sang the perks of gym-trimmed physiques, quite a shift for a population whose main means of transportation is their own two feet. People speak English in whatever accent they learned it, so we were treated to a Ghanaian reciting the rote emergency procedures with Mandarin musicality.

Was the lone Caucasian male next to me a missionary or mercenary? Or *both*. He sat with all the ease of someone who's killed before and gotten away scot-free.

We landed during "cool" season with temperatures topping 100 degrees.

On the road, we passed *ashawos* (prostitutes) that locals claim are all Nigerians, while the street hustlers are labeled Malian. This is a displacement of blame often echoed elsewhere.

Plainclothes police mingle with pistols in their trouser pockets protruding like hard-ons, and single women forced to carry all burdens on their head weave between buildings marked in chalk for demolition.

How do you build an economy? Redundancy. The opposite of downsizing and job slashing. We watched twenty men stand around at midnight putting up a Christmas tree, a task that could have easily been done by two.

Some of the cheesiest music I've ever heard is in taxis through-out Africa—Lounge Jazz lite and diabetic-shock pop preening. Taste is not a heritage.

But it's the muscles you can't see that matter in a fight, the smaller, neglected ones. It is best to aim never to cross people—especially anyone who cooks your food, cuts your hair or sleeps beside you.

Ghana struggles with its own north/south divide.

I've often wondered: What is the tensile limit of cohesion cultur-ally? How far can geography stretch—scaled for cities and nations—before a culture fractures?

This northern zone was a wellspring of the Blues, a land where they emanated and never left.

Still buzzed at 9 a.m. on *Pito* (millet beer) from the night before, the *fra fra* quartet proclaimed that they play better when they are drunk. This was telling as they seemed plenty wasted already.

On the dusty-road outskirts of Tamale near the School of Hygiene, the group prefer the name given to their tribe by colonialists (*fra fra*) rather than having decreed what to correct after the fact, a retraction made on their behalf.

The group is led by Small, a man who celebrates his diminutive size rather than seeing it as lack. He picked the two-string "guitar" with dog-tags fastened at the head as rattles.

As funeral songs are often done in procession, I took the mics to the group since they seemed reluctant to enter the compound. Instead, they gyrated in circles on the gravel outside. In recording, coverage is more important than precision. Every microphone tells a slightly dif-ferent version of the truth, so I quickly threw up as many as possible.

Rather than resembling deathly dirges, these were largely celebrations.

As so often is the case, literacy no way interfered with creativity. Small was able to riff almost endlessly. In fact, his performances grew freer and stronger past the ten-minute mark, so much so that songs became nearly different tunes entirely. Following his flow, I simply let tape roll as long as possible until things fell apart, but even then I feared that still greater things may've lay beyond if only they musi-cians had kept going.

A hallmark of fra fra culture are the tiny, bone mouth-flutes that they call "horns," since that is what they are made from.

When we were through, Small asserted that he could see that music was "in my blood." But I protested.

Music is in all of us. Rhythm must run through our very veins to carry life.

Using the Only Filter I Knew

My mother moved west from Kansas's edge to agricultural pre–Silicon Valley back when San Jose's population was thousands, not millions. The first day, she smiled wide and greeted a passing neighbor on the street. They said nothing in return. This was the only time my mother had ever experienced this in her life. It sent her home ill. But quickly she grew accustomed. An early strain of autism had already set upon the land.

Over time, if you stay away long enough your homeland becomes a foreign country.

Both my parents were Depression-era babies. They raised us to fear scarcity. Most of all, amid abundance.

My mother was a coupon-cutting crusader—often for items she would've otherwise not desired.

Growing up, my understanding was that rich people were something that only existed on TV. They were as make-believe as Bigfoot or Starsky & Hutch.

But soon Reagan rolled east, breaching the beltway. It was then that the elite came to life—the greed unleashed.

No longer satisfied to pull the strings from afar, the gentry lunged to the foreground, displacing the middlemen to themselves become the stars.

VI.

LOSING THE HUMAN RACE:

Compartmentalization Coffins

35

Living Downstream
of the Slush

If black lives truly mattered, hardly a soul would listen to Justin Timberlake. Instead, he inexplicably has filled stadiums.

Agency is something that is systematically denied the poor, whose art is deemed born of tradition, never modern.

Some justice arrives whenever the colonized come to colonize the colonizers culturally—Indians hooking the British on tea and *nan*, African-Americans entraining slave traders to polyrhythm.

The working class has lost—or had stolen—its music and, therefore, its voice. The occasional artist that miraculously rises from poverty is quickly assimilated and then held up as false proof of a meritocracy.

But the gargantuan and escalating volume of content sets celebrity as the default to distinguish art. Nepotism remains the closest a narcissist can come to altruism.

The elite exude and epitomize the ultimate endowment: the expectation of being denied nothing. Most of all, victimhood and underdog status—self-professed outsiderism. The apex of advantage is not having to admit that you're *advantaged,* and that the entire game was rigged from the start.

36

Without You,
Nothing

What would the sound track to modern life have been without African-Americans?

Certainly lots of waltzes.

And no banjo.

"American music" *is* African music. Not just Rap, Soul, Blues, and Jazz, but Rock, and even Bluegrass and largely Country, too.

Music, like almost all post-industrial endeavor, is bent by the prism of Hollywoodization. What "roots" musician does not have latent Sam Peckinpah and John Ford images swirling inside his head?

Rather than racial romanticization, I am a firm believer in power residing within individuals, not groups or lineages. (After all, the drummer on *Thriller* was a white man.)

But if anything, I am a *black* supremacist. It is difficult not to bow down before a culture that gave birth to the Gospel, Blues, *and* Jazz—the nuclei of all popular music that has followed. The contribution of slide guitar, muted trumpet, slap bass, 4/4 backbeat, and bent third-notes—or any one alone—stand mightily enough to give pause.

37

Mixed-Up Tapes

If someone claims that they are the least racist person that you will ever meet, you know that you are in the presence of the most racist motherfucker you'll ever know.

For people often are most defined by what they disown.

When people proclaim that my daughter is mixed-race, my question is: "Mixed with what?" For we are only one race. Are they suggesting that somehow an extraterrestrial or different species found its way into the mix somewhere down the line?

Rwandan-Bergamasque-Celtic-White-Trash Californian?

If they feel the urge to go to such lengths of specification, then this mouthful would be far more on target.

Hatred in all forms has ignorance as its root. Because to truly know someone as an individual and celebrate their complexity—both the good and not-so-good characteristics—renders hate virtually impossible to sustain.

Hate ultimately consumes the hateful. It leaves one straddled with the illusion of significant difference, keeping us apart. Stalin purged his country's doctors. Then his own health failed when there was no one competent to care for him left in his kingdom.

But a hateful state is something we can maybe work with—passion just awaiting rechanneling. It is with indifference and apathy where there is little hope, in those cesspools of cynicism. Similarly, it is not the one who is explicitly threatening that we need worry most about. They are ultimately providing a warning, a cry for help. More ominous are those who deny their emotions entirely, refusing to share any feeling at all.

38

Leading by Disguise

James Brown and Michael Jackson arguably did as much for racial progress in America as Martin Luther King Jr and Malcolm X.

But modeling Black Panther Party berets at halftime during the Super Bowl is not a revolutionary act. It is more an empty mockery.

We've entered the age of pop protest, politics used as stage props for consumeristic-propaganda disposable mouthpieces.

You can't be radical *and* a billionaire. Such is a worst case of wanting to have your cake and eat it, too. Nor is it possible to genuinely condemn violence while benefitting grossly from a system based on economic unfairness—for one person to have multiple homes around the globe, scores of others must go homeless and/or hungry entirely.

Same shit, different millennium.

True insurgency is not the aspiration to benefit from a system of inequality, but to *destroy* it.

An Immigrant in Your Own Hometown

To find the nuance and spirit of a place you have to drive past the gravitational pull of its touristic center. The commercialized stratum is ditched the farther you travel from any international airport.

We recorded far up a gravel road in a Sardegna ruin from 2000 BC. It was a rocky spiral with surprisingly nonreflective sound—utterly insulated in a way that foam and baffles could never achieve. Having to duck horizontally to clear the low and lone entrance, I misgauged the height and rammed myself three steps backwards—my cranium no match for the building's three-foot-thick boulders.

The polyglot artist reportedly could play percussion before speaking a word. When hearing his mother's John Lee Hooker 8-tracks, he was confused at English being sung and would ask, "Mom, why is this Tunisian man singing in that funny language?"

To this day he is checked in on almost daily in his father's family's village by the Italian anti-terrorism police.

Being an EU passport-holder is of diminished value when its credibility is doubted even when displayed. Similarly, Marilena once had a border patrol agent in Amsterdam crease and attempt to scratch off her picture as if it were phony. When that failed, he tried testing her by naming a nonexistent Italian region to see if she could be tricked into mistakenly affirming it. All this before he finally relented and allowed her to enter her fatherland.

Sadly, the recordings in Sardegna stalled. The artist held on to guitar-god aesthetics like armor, too tightly to be free.

39

More White Guys with Guitars: the remake of the prequel to "A fine line between love and take"

Thievery is *not* the sincerest form of flattery.

African music's second transatlantic journey whitewashed it by way of England. Meanwhile, in almost direct and concurrent correspondence, most African-Americans abandoned Rock as no longer their own.

Despite the common claim, Bob Dylan was not the one who brought serious lyrics to rock-era pop music.

Chuck Berry did. He was specializing in story songs almost a decade before fanboy Dylan ever stepped foot in Greenwich Village.

Adding sting is how much Berry was ostracized by black audiences for dabbling in what was commonly viewed as white hillbilly music—a classic case of ethnic-consent attempting to blockade progress.

Relatedly, personal diversification and flexibility—the knack to evolve and change—is an honor that is hoarded. Bowie and Madonna could flip identities routinely, but those of African parentage are generally pigeonholed and depreciated. Lest we forget, Little Richard was wearing blush, lip gloss, and eyeliner decades before Bowie, Boy George, and KISS.

By the 1970s, mainstream black artists had been relegated almost exclusively to singing-roles only. Hendrix was held up by my peers as an exception to the rule, instead of *the rule*. In one generation, mass-media machinations had managed to confuse and conceal the unmatched instrumental mastery of Charlie Parker, Art Blakey, Thelonious Monk, and James Jamerson, to name a few of the *any*.

Perhaps Elvis's greatest sin of assimilation was not musical but rather having the audacity to simulate being strung up and whipped barebacked in his bad-boy star vehicle *Jailhouse Rock*. With that one act, he appropriated hundreds of years of torture for his own self-glorification as an outsider, recontextualizing his home state's holocaust of slavery.

Elvis's hometown held the horror of a reported three to four hundred African-Americans having been hanged one night in mass. The lore was that Tupelo was thereafter cursed. From those ashes, the King rose.

That so much of American music was created by refugees fleeing persecution *within* America makes it all the more awe-inspiring—secular sound sanctified.

40

Can't Hold a Tune?

The great treason of most "World Music" is a lack of tunes—the hidden message being that the majority of international artists are not sage enough to compose at high levels. Instead, the emphasis is placed squarely on Flavor of the Month, fly-by-night exoticness or forced zaniness versus depth.

But exoticism alone isn't enough. In the end it's just another pose. The basic clichés run roughly as follows ...

a) Africa: rhythmic
b) Eastern Europe: whacky, maniacal energy
c) Middle East/Asia: mystical

Gatekeepers in the West tend to prefer their exoticness strained through European values, laundered and starched by capitalism. They wear style like a toupee, even walking with British, French, German, or American accents.

The buried signifier is that foreign artists only work from the tradition of "their people" and not out of individuality.

Calling trailblazing artists like Konono No. 1 "World Music" is no different than claiming Run-DMC are Country & Western simply because they come from America.

This quagmire is only deepened by the cheap retreat of lackluster artists that stoop to hiding behind their ethnicity, pimping-out parentage (e.g., the "I'm like them" stance). They act as double agents—partners towards greater blandness.

Music can be contaminated by commercialism regardless of its lack of sales. If the intention was to achieve popularity with an imaginary audience versus art sparking from the need to communicate directly with specific people, then it has been adulterated. Failure should not exonerate, nor obscurity indicate artfulness.

What is missed is how much cross-fertilization occurs. Reggae and Rap ricocheted back to Africa. Even more overlooked is how the biggest disseminator of music on the continent has been religion—choral arrangements pirated by nineteenth-century crusaders. Their influence continues dribbling down today.

41

Boxed within Borders

Asking a member of the urban gentry in the world's poorest nations to speak on behalf of their countrymen is equivalent to taking Ivanka Trump's or a Kardashian's word that the kids in America are doing all right.

When it comes to the 1%, every nation has them—even the poorest places on the globe. And the result is one 1% talking to another and then deciding what the truth is for everybody else.

When Master Mun Hai in Cambodia dared perform once in the capital, he was told his music was "cowshit." He smelled like a peasant, they jeered, fit for singing to livestock only. He left the city, shaken. It was years before he picked up an instrument again.

An illustration of how much imbalance there is in wealth globally is the number-one poorest nation being literally *twice* as poor as the tenth poorest. Even at the bottom, there is stunning inequity—different shades of *grave*.

People speak of dystopian futures where technology will create an immortal class. But in part, this already exists on a planet where life expectancies are halved for the most economically impoverished nations, simply by the accident of birthplace.

Rumors have long run about the development of sonics as a military device—the alleged "brown tone" that can bring down buildings. But such aggressive and obvious an apparatus is not needed. The nerve gas of robotized, generic soundscapes has already descended, placating subjects into submission.

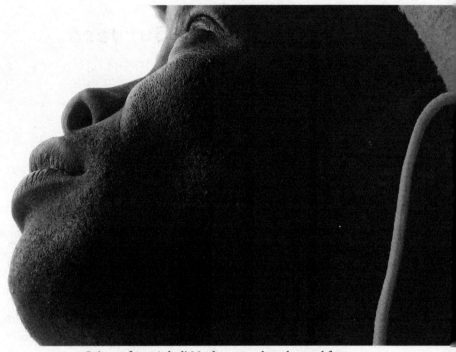

Gaitano from Acholi Machon searches skyward for
relief for the world's newest nation, South Sudan.

South Sudan:
Selective Freedom

South Sudan is the newest nation in the world. And like many youngsters, it is a troubled one plagued by growing pains.

The dueling lokembe players of Acholi Machon have thumbs the size of compulsive texters. Their instruments are made in a range of sizes—from toy-box to a yard long. When played in unison they act as a piano diced into pieces.

The leader, Gaitano—a diminutive, but taut man—approaches every conversation as a confrontation. He is someone who has known loss all too well. Every "hello" feels like a reproach. His macho manner is betrayed only by stray sashays when hurried.

His partner, Cornelio, wears a perpetually weary "what now" expression and prefers to let the music do the talking. The members call themselves "diggers," the term that they use for the farming which they were born into and still subsist on.

What they and so many lack is a basic right: a freedom to move. The liberty to travel is guaranteed by Article 13 of the United Nations Declaration of Human Rights. But these privileges are applied oh so selectively. The luxury to literally become airborne is something that even the possession of a passport from all but a handful of elite countries, does not automatically nor easily grant.

Without an embassy in their own country, Acholi Machon were forced to travel to Kenya—not for an interview, but simply for the minutes-long process of physically handing over their passports and having fingerprints taken. This excursion was the first time they'd ever traveled outside of their country. Along the way, officers at the Uganda border extorted money for the passage and a Nairobi guest house bilked them hundreds for a room that should have been a few dollars.

Worse, after their first application was refused, they were forced to repeat this entire odyssey a second time.

They were labeled "aspiring immigrants" even though the duo were middle-aged, knew not a word of English, are both long married and have fifteen children between them. Even more relevantly, they specialize writing anthems like "Acholi Land Is Good Land for Staying," a celebration of the independence that they and their fellow citizens fought to achieve for almost half a century. None of this was enough to deter misplaced paranoia from the authorities.

As Keut Ran from the Khmer Rouge Survivors flew for the first time, she feared she was going to the moon. "Why are you so far, England?" she cried. Her visa had been denied on the first try, also, keeping the country safe from a blind, sixty-seven-year-old grandmother who was unable to speak one word of English—as anti- of a threat as could be found.

Personally, I have been delayed twice at the USA border after officers find South Sudan stamped in my passport. This has happened ever since the country of Sudan was placed on a list of countries that trigger a second inspection.

The issue is that I have never been to Sudan in my life, and South Sudan could not be further apart philosophically from their former rulers to the north. The southerners battled decades for independence from Sudan and are as distinct ideologically as North and South Korea. But as much as I try to stress this to the border patrol agents, their reply has consistently been an uncomprehending, "Yes. Sudan. South *Sudan*." Even those whose job it is to know better are prone to confusion.

42

Debunk the Funk

Despite the best Caucasian intentions and aspirations, if I let go of my daughter's hand and take two steps back, through that single cowardly act I am free and instantly washed clean of her ancestry.

But she cannot escape. It is an involuntarily inclusion, with no escape.

I sliced my chin open at age two trying to be like my father. My face slathered in shaving cream, I snuck to the bathroom, and wielded a safety razor that wasn't so safe after all.

Still today, I bear the scars and follow in his footsteps even when running away.

Though not a gay man, I have been closeted—hiding feelings and denying true desires that defied my existing commitments, living a secret life inside my head. I was raised that the worst sin was speaking unpleasant emotional truths. It became my duty to protect others from reality. But having been coached to take care of others more than myself, I inflicted far greater harm.

Being too "nice" is, in fact, not nice at all.

Most of the best songs and intentions throughout history get lost, trapped within that person's being, an inch from liberty, but still unable to ever reach the world.

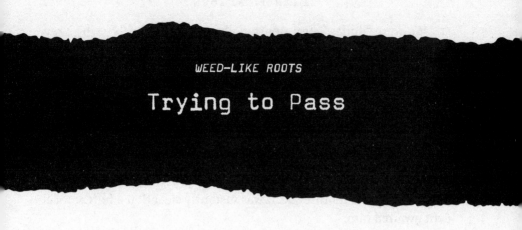

Trying to Pass

In the suburbs where I grew up, you could drive around for hours without seeing a single thing built before you were born. And if it was built prior, it was just years before. This made the very place we were most oriented to, disorienting nonetheless.

And drive we did. For hours. "Cruising," as it was called, before becoming outlawed entirely. That term's gay-bar meaning had failed to reach even the few miles over the coastal hills to the "wrong" side of the bay.

The DNA of some places is so strong that if you see even one block of it, you know the whole. Other places are so dilute that everyone's experience differs and there is little "there" there.

From such a place is where I sprang.

The streets were hemmed-in by homes so flimsy that though they were brand-new, they radiated random noises, phantom pleas. Our town had only one place for travelers to stay, a single shitty motel. It stood as proof that where we lived, no one really wanted to be. Most ended up there only through accident or compromise.

It's a stomping ground for cartoon-proportioned and obsessively tattooed boys and girls resembling blowup dolls, bouncing around within raised, window-tinted SUVs. Lives lived as checklists—prescribed monthly haircuts, migrating piercings, the latest-generation phones, pimped-out rides, and lovers or children worn like accessories—every detail a bit too impeccably preset. Inevitably, militarized civilians fight each other—over parking spaces, words and gaze, discounted devices—divided by stoked and amplified fears.

We were "dudes"—unintentionally and unironically—who grew up amid Disco's backlash, headbanging to stave off any hint of dance or femininity. Affections were limited to fist bumps and half hugs. Calling each other by last name only, even verbally keeping each other at arm's length.

One friend's motto was "I'm going to either fuck or fight someone tonight." That he ended up taking his own life decades later, in hindsight, seems sadly like a foregone conclusion.

Another bequeathed me with pseudo-psychic powers when he bought himself a motorcycle. It was instantly clear that a horrific accident awaited him.

We blasted the loudest music we could find—simultaneously a proclamation of rage and a prayer for connection. Teenage rocketships, we attempted liftoff but could not yet manage to pull free and reach orbit from the gravity of our fractured, nuclear families. Years later, most of us would clutch to remnants of our youthful selves—the fuselage—images that remained, and maybe always were, visible only to us.

It didn't matter if certain records had gone platinum a half dozen times over, we were the only ones within miles that knew the words, or so we believed. We chanted them like secret handshakes.

We were unwanted but not unloved. Society had simply neglected to allow room for us during the days of the Cold War economic bonanza. Generation X were casualties of the Baby Boomers' self-absorption, displaced by the first generation ever to refuse surrendering adolescence to make way for the oncoming generation.

Standing at the Border, Longing for Home: Just Another Brick in the Wall

You could've spat on the USA from there.

Just a one-lane expressway and some plywood and tarp lean-tos stood squashed before the border.

These were the people our president and armed militias fear— Honduran refugees and hate-crime victims, families huddled in camping tents on the ground.

Most seemed so despondent and underfed that rising to their feet proved a burden, let alone scaling a barbed-wire fence four times their own height.

It forces one to ponder how bad where they are running from must be that they are willing to endure this as an alternative.

José, a scrawny teenage sketch artist, left due to the gay bashing that he'd seen claim other lives.

Similarly, a transgender women had suffered multiple attacks along the way from Central America that only echoed what'd driven her north to begin with. She bore a heart tattoo like a bull's-eye on her chest.

Another man wore a poncho and never removed his hands from beneath. He arched back as if defense had become his default posture. Surveillance cameras stared down at us, sporting mohawks of rusty nails placed to discourage pigeons from landing.

One boy who feared his photo being taken would somehow inter- fere with his chances for passage to the states, advised that the gov- ernment should "tear down the walls inside your heart."

Not a single resident raised their voice loudly enough to register on the LED meter. Even when taken to a far corner near the lone bathroom shared by over one hundred people, their whispers could not compete with the city's noise floor. But the one theme all of their stories shared was "violence."

On the surrounding blocks, diversity denied by stereotypes is found—Haitian hurricane immigrants mingling freely in the city that welcomed them after America continued to hold a grudge against the only nation ever formed in history by slaves that successfully over-threw their masters. This influx of newcomers will assuredly infuse vibrancy, in the same way that Chinese immigrants came to reshape the border town of Mexicali, making it culinarily unlike any other area throughout Mexico.

The city is often dubbed "TJ" by southern California frat boys that use it as their misogynist lap-dance playground. It was labeled "dangerous" by the college-age daughter of liberal friends. She'd been raised just over an hour's drive north but had never actually stepped foot there.

Though we'd been waved through without a glance while enter-ing from the States, a nearly five-hour stop-and-go queue awaited us heading home—evidence of the clear trade deficit between sides.

43

Wide Privilege

I can never really know what true discrimination is. Aside from childhood fat-ism, I've only experienced it secondhand.

Seeing my sister leered and jeered at due to her Down syndrome spawned almost every (failed) fistfight of my early years.

Today, decades later, a continent away, I watch cars slow for my mother-in-law—a senior citizen crippled from polio. Her skin color has been so sexualized within Italy that daring to walk down the street is seen as an invitation, an assumption of availability.

Recently, I copped an attitude with a border patrol agent. And then I was allowed to walk away, entering the USA without a hitch. Before I'd even left his sight, shame overcame me. The leeway that I breathed as if it were a given and normal state was suddenly smothering. This was followed by a surge of panic that the officer would come to his senses and change his mind before the escalator I'd stepped onto fully descended.

That I can recall, I've been pulled over four times without being handed a citation. Additionally, I've been ticketed on at least a half dozen occasions and was never once asked to step out of the car. At most I was delayed ten minutes, but more likely not even five.

Not liking privilege doesn't change benefitting from it regardless. It does not absolve. I take for granted being able to express myself freely and not be shot in the process—a right that is bestowed, but unconscionably not shared by all.

Selective sounds have been made outlaw—my raised voice is

deemed legal, while others' silence is potentially perceived as defiance or even menace.

By birth, I am among America's "Most *un*-Wanted Men"—assumed innocent even though proven guilty.

44

What Can You Say?

Acquaintances often ask, "What's Africa like?"

Even from our meager travels, the sheer breadth is humbling. The only single word I can try to muster is: diverse.

Multiculturalism didn't begin centuries after citizens of the African continent were forcibly relocated. It already existed long before, at home.

Another recurring question: "Is it nice there?"

The answer for there and anywhere is the same.

"Do people live there and call it home? Then, yes, it must be quite nice. Nicer than we can ever really know."

VII.

WE FIRST:

Rising above Compulsive Competitiveness

45

All That Is Not Singing Is Merely Chatter

Singing-contest shows churn song into cage fights.

Art was once a refuge from the compulsive competitiveness of capitalistic society's intrusion into family and daily life.

Growing up, as outsiders we loathed the jocks. Music was a revolt against their male-domineering ilk. To see sports mentality increasingly pervert music is tragic indeed. As part propaganda program, twenty-four-hour sports channels now make it seem as if there is never any relent from rivalry. It's not just for Sundays anymore.

An overly individuated society leads to an obsession with biography—"great man" dissertations of history versus the collective efforts that gradually shape culture.

I was raised in the paradigm that proper indoctrination into boyhood required having a favorite sports team, a dream car—lists at the ready—as opposed to simply not caring much at all.

I was taught to shoot a gun while crossing the salt flats of northern Nevada. Too small to lift the pistol without using both hands, all I remember is the crinkled hiss and ping of my missing shots as we idled by the roadside.

Popular culture was the one relatively untrodden path where misfits could excel ... or at least not suck.

We were left alone to battle emptiness.

46

Go Get Othered

It should nearly be a duty for everyone to experience outsiderness. Travel all but ensures this to happen. You have not really lived until someone has talked shit in front of you, feeling that license has been conferred due to language difference, coupled with the basic assumption that you are clearly more than a tad on the slow side for not understanding what they are saying to begin with.

Movement upends perception. Important things can recede—families and commitments forgotten. And little random occurrences magnify, sometimes ineradicably.

Through music, the Malawi Mouse men open a
window to their rural experiences.

Malawi Mouse Boys (the sequel): Score for a Film about Malawi without Music from Malawi

Colonialism continued in cultural form.

The first thing they noticed was the funny way the foreigners spoke Chichewa. It rang untrue.

That the most notable accomplishment of the man cast as the tribal chief was playing a butler on a nineties laugh-tracked sitcom should've already been a giveaway. After all, there are only mere hundreds of actual chiefs to be found throughout Malawi. Certainly, not one of them could have been right for the small speaking part.

The Malawi Mouse Boys had been invited to attempt a score for the first feature film ever from their nation.

But after writing and recording hours of music at their own expense, the filmmakers without explanation opted instead to use an "experienced" composer with no ties whatsoever to Malawi. In fact, he's never stepped foot even once in Africa.

This composer hails from a famous family in his own nation, a country which ranks as a powerhouse economy —a sharp contrast to Malawi consistently falling among the ten poorest nations on earth. Despite the best of intentions, the colonialist model continues to endure—African artists too often viewed as mere source material that European experts are then needed to improve upon and make presentable.

Make no mistake, the filmmakers' aesthetic intention was in no way surrealistic or ironic. They were meticulously concerned with authenticity and accuracy in other details. They wouldn't dream of dressing the protagonist in a powdered Elizabethan wig or having the cast suddenly burst out chatting Lithuanian but featuring the most cliché of all African instruments—the *kora*—was inexcusably indulged. Doing so is the equivalent of Scottish bagpipes being incorporated in a film about Israel. The kora hails from Senegal and Mali—almost four thousand miles away from Malawi—the distance of driving across the USA, *twice.*

Worse, the film defaults to using symphonic music, the ultimate sonic symbol of Eurocentrism, Western dominance and its supposed superiority. The white composer wrote while noodling on a kora he'd picked up for the first time, an instrument traditionally passed down through Griot family lineage only, a sacred birthright, consuming a lifetime to master.

The bitter irony is that the film itself depicts a biographical tale of a young man from rural Malawi who through his own wits saved his family and village from famine—an arc that mirrors the Malawi Mouse Boys' story and what they've managed to achieve with their own music.

Only the Mouse Boys' living conditions are even *more* impoverished. In fact, it was striking that when reviewing the film's footage they felt that the character's plight was unremarkable, "clean," average—"rich," not poor.

Through music, they have reached the world—releasing internationally the first popular music album ever in Chichewa. This led to their triumphing at Peter Gabriel's WOMAD Festival in Great Britain (their CDs outselling even those by headliner Gilberto Gil), followed by tours of Australia, New Zealand, and the USA.

Nonetheless, they continue to battle poverty. Their success has been a double-edged sword. The income has allowed them certain improvements—tin roofs for their homes, air mattresses rather than dirt floors that their children can sleep on, English lessons, and the purchase of a sound system and generator. But it has not been enough to end their struggle and suffering. Locals refuse to employ them now as they resent and even ridicule that the group members have traveled abroad since they consequently do not believe that the group are in need of jobs or worthy of assistance.

Therefore, to survive the men continue to sell mice shish kebabs by the roadside to travelers. They also now have resorted to hawking charcoal. The creation of this charcoal involves many of the same hazards as mouse hunting—exposure to wild boars, poisonous snakes, and spiders. But also, in this case, smoke inhalation. It demands that they hike into the distant hills since the forest has receded stratospherically from clear-cutting. They then have to locate and burn down a tree, wait until it smolders, and then chop up and gather the remains. They then haul the chunks back many kilometers to home. Each load requires multiple days' labor and spreads filth. If they are lucky, they will sell the lot for around a dollar. Recently, Mulligo was nearly crushed when a trunk overturned atop him.

The Malawi Mouse Boys' music for the film was born of the local earth. They used found materials from their village—a smashed spoke, water buckets, their handmade four-string guitar, a jar, bamboo horns, a machete, wind, insects trapped in jars, an alpha monkey's call, shovel scrapes, a faulty transistor radio, and the ground itself. It is Zero Kilometer music, paralleling the film's story.

A donated Fender six-string was dragged through the dirt for texture, but Mulligo was more than displeased that its backside bore superficial scratches. Plastic bag strands had attached themselves like ticks to his clay-and-thatch outhouse—materialism setting-in, literally and figuratively.

In contrast to the group's often sunny music, this is the most brooding and baroque material that they've ever produced—a meditation on having faced famine repeatedly.

Out of desperation, two of the four members have now fled to South Africa in the hopes of work. It is a journey fraught with hazard as Malawians are often accused of "stealing" jobs and regarded in Cape Town as an invading force in much the same way that Latinos and other "aliens" are too often viewed in the United States.

Sir Ian McKellan has pointed out that though fifty-two actors have been Oscar-nominated for portraying LGBT characters, no openly gay actor has ever won an Academy Award. Most media continues to fall a far cry from midcentury Italian neorealist ideals of casting an actual Calabrian truck driver if the character called for *is* a Calabrian truck driver.

The argument here is not for charity, but balance. When faced with two gifted artists, those least likely to be represented otherwise should be given the nod. That diversification of participation can only benefit humanity as a whole.

The millionaire British-born director's own parents' west African ancestry acted as a buffer to closer scrutiny and insight regarding how insensitively the dynamic was handled.

Hopefully, any failure to draw talent locally will someday be looked upon with as much disdain as bygone cowboy and Indian films casting Sicilian immigrants in headdresses as Native Americans.

Demoralized, the band remained determined that the music be heard, so a humble digital release was made.

Whether their score is a more elegant and fitting soundtrack for a film about overcoming hunger in Malawi is now for the listener to decide.

Life Lived like a
Suicide Hotline Call

About the only thing we had in common was blood. But that was enough.

I would have killed in his defense.

You can sleep inches from someone the first decade and a half of your life—memorizing their breath and the way they turn—and still not know them.

At Yellowstone Park, my older brother once leapt over a safety railing to stand at the very edge of an enormous waterfall's crest.

Always having struggled to articulate his feelings, he was asking us a question: Did we care?

But our screams were drowned beside the water's force.

As my only brother stood one misstep from death, a current bigger than both of us pulsed and pounded, spraying mist about his silhouette like an aura. Beneath his mock smile I could see a deeper hurt crystalizing.

He was also making a statement.

"I am in pain and not sure my life is not worth risking. For anything . . . or maybe even for nothing at all."

Less successful than he was at navigating the young-boy gauntlet of sports and shit-talking, it was I that had been the fortunate one.

Stumbling upon art, I'd found a path away from jock culture's monochromaticism and firewalls, providing some makings for a richer emotional vocabulary. It gave me something to tether to. Music provided a sanctuary where fears could be expressed with (slightly) lessened fear, a safety valve for angst, longing, and doubt that shredded lives among our milieu's nearly nonverbal males who'd tried their damnedest to raise us "right."

They were elders that blew smoke rings in our face as a way to educate and when challenged held us down until we screamed their proper name, "Uncle!"—proof of their supremacy, evidence that they existed. They preferred engines to music, shutting off the radio to listen instead to their V8's roar as they drove.

My brother's rage acted as a paternity test.

Most people are murdered by something from inside themselves, not the boogeymen they fear.

The true boogeyman is you.

It is hard labor to kill oneself—a near full-time job.

My uncles would play games of roulette with beer can pull-tabs, dropping the shards of metal inside each twelve-ounce can before gulping it down. It was a practice they persisted in until too many resulting deaths forced the manufacturers to design openers that could no longer detach.

Many toil day after day with excess—cigarettes, alcohol, gluttony, recklessness, passivity—but still their bodies will not succumb, enduring decades of degradation.

My kin bled internally from primordial wounds. Maybe only drops a day, but never fully healed.

47

Affectation Containers: Something's Missing

The people with the best voices are often the most awful singers—belting at the top of their lungs and range about ... *nada*. This in the same way that a tall person might not excel at basketball or every husky comer make a good linebacker.

Most commercialized singers are Bermuda Triangles emotionally, pumped up on steroidal sentiment. You cannot find them. They act as living holograms.

Instead, vocalists that enrich us encode emotion. They sing the subtext more than the text, from deep within the throat and asking for no reward beyond the song. And through what is implied, they deconstruct and rewrite entire tunes.

Tom Petty's pleading "heys" were kissing cousins to mariachi "ay-yai-yai" *gritos*—the juncture that feeling continues past where mere words fail, much the same way that Gospel choirs' cadence acts as a continuation of the preacher's incantations.

If one is oppressed, the voiced but unspoken elements become primary means of communication—beneath the radar, undetected or at least not fully deciphered.

Usually the more meaningful an action, the less conscious an actor is of it. Words are most likely to deceive due to their intentionally trying to "tell" you something. Contrarily, the feet are known as the most honest part of the body: they are located the furthest from the head.

With time, people's posture begins to reveal who they truly are—how they've used or not used their bodies, the emotions most frequently expressed (and repressed) become etched in each face.

48

Binary Thinking and the Perpetuation of Cycles of Abuse

Proclaiming that Lady Gaga or some other privileged person "has talent" demonstrates the same lack of nuance and recognition of continuums that keeps people stuck in abusive relationships.

Yes, someone "*can* be nice," but that doesn't mean that person *is* nice. Certainly, not so much that they are worthy of intimacy and care beyond the scads of consistently kind people.

This is not a claim that nearly anyone is without some merit. But glimmers of virtue do not even come close to justifying that person's domination over others with equal or even stronger ability.

If all questions are structured as false dichotomies—in which someone is either good or bad—then any room for progress is made nearly impossible. In such an oversimplified framework, one has either passed or failed. Only when we willingly acknowledge our flaws—our humanness—does the potential to grow become possible.

Serbian expat Matić Miroslav proves that not all
buskers are created equal.

After the Bombing Has Stopped, Don't Let Your Women Go to Kosovo

Wandering the sepia-toned blonde streaked streets of Ljubljana on a Sunday morning I ran across a busker, Matić Miroslav. He'd smoked so much in his lifetime that his lips seemed as if they were dangling a lit cigarette between his lips even though he wasn't.

Though he'd yet to play a note of music, there was a regal dignity in his posture—as well as a downright badass-ness—tipoffs that he was the real deal.

Peace had long come to the splintered land that once was Yugoslavia, but Matić remained adrift, the war still reverberating within him.

Like most Cold War–forged Americans, I sometimes lapse into Eastern Bloc thinking, regarding such an immense region as monolithic. Yugoslavia's having splintered into seven different countries (across an area merely the size of Oregon) stands alone as proof of the tremendous diversity that exists there.

Matić stood past an alleyway window-display of paled vinyl-single covers from the 1960s and 1970s—face after face that'd tasted provincial fame for a hit (or maybe two) before subsiding.

Bowed one-stringed instruments like Matić's dot the globe, not so much because of any direct pedigree but due to their very rudimentariness making them a near inevitability. This is in much the same way that flat bread and frame drums are found almost everywhere, with each region claiming theirs as the seminal one.

As Matić and I struggled to communicate, by some cosmic miracle, a young Serbian that Matić had never met passed, offering to translate.

An agreement was made to record some songs. Mr. Miroslav proceeded to offer a set of music and spoken word. Not a soul stopped to listen. The impulsive session was only interrupted when the church tower rang for Sunday mass. He stood, pointed towards the service that was calling him, performed a sloppy sign of the cross, and then departed—scampering towards the bells.

I was left on the metal bridge, its railings bent beneath the weight of lovers' padlocks, still clinging long after promises broken.

49

Fight for Your Right
Not to Fight

Neofascist Hardcore was inspired by the Bad Brains, whose every member was black. "Good ol' boy" Southern rock's template was cast by the "interracial" Allman Brothers. And possibly the most he-man of musical forms, Thrash Metal was pioneered and popularized by Metallica, whose lead guitarist is of Filipino descent. Meanwhile, White Power skinheads in England co-opted their uniform from Jamaican "rude boys," a fashion of Levi's 501s which were themselves invented by a Jewish immigrant. Hypocrisies like these are hard to outdo.

Some jihadist kid with too much testosterone pumping through his brain dons his favorite UK soccer club jersey and blasts American rap moments before unleashing a terror attack. Somehow he is able to compartmentalize all of that cultural confusion. Such is the result of the psyche and emotion being harshly segregated.

The relationship we have with extremism is a codependent one. The more it is fought, the more justified and radicalized they become.

Kill one terrorist, indoctrinate three more. The math is marred, for the targeted number is not finite.

Violence is not a deterrent. It's a stalling tactic.

Much harder, though, is to hate someone that you are dancing with.

Teenage attitude is a hard thing to cover up, even if you try.

Yemen:
I Am a Good Person and
So Is My Friend

Yemen fits like a puzzle piece into the Horn of Africa, at the exact point where they split apart.

The heat was stifling, and our shirts were wrung with sweat. During each take we turned off the "Made in Pakistan" ceiling fans—branded *Pac Fan*, rather than Pac Man. Asking the musicians to not smoke on the breaks was clearly as rude as asking them not to breathe.

Anwar played his *oud* with a plastic picnic knife and what he described as his saddest song sounded the happiest.

Our driver had never been to that part of town and though he passes the inlet from the main road twice daily, commented disdainfully that he "never even knew that shacks like this existed in *our* city."

Stuck in colonial-period taunts, the kids kept calling me "Johnny." One asked if I was *galle*. The musicians lied and told him, no, I was an Arab since they said that I could somehow pass for a "light one." The sun had long set and this lie would offer me safe passage as we trekked the dirt cul-de-sac while hauling a hundred pounds of gear. A husky Yemeni boy offered a moonwalk tribute as we trudged onward and a man with a hatchet deliberately chipped holes in a newly stuccoed wall, crafting a design.

They assured us of the obvious: that being *galle* (non-Muslim) "*always!*" possessed a negative connotation.

Most brutality is based on confusion. The confusion that someone is worse than they are or that they play a more significant role in your life than they actually do. But no matter how psychotic and paranoid an individual's thought processes might be, if what they believed were in fact true, their behavior would make perfect sense after all.

When recording with Tinariwen in southeast Algeria at the end of 2010, residents were alarmed by a flock of recent arrivals throughout the region who spoke Arabic with "strange accents." It was ISIS back when they were still just a local band.

Here people make fun of Texan soldiers spitting snuff. Instead, the locals stuff their cheek full of *khat*, until it drizzles down their beard.

With three sisters and their respective families trapped back home—partitioned by just a ten-mile inlet that might as well be galaxies—Anwar wrote a ten-minute song specially for us titled "Why (the War)?"

It is a question I fear that no one can answer.

So Malnourished of Love, You Ate Your Own Heart

As the quality of sound went up, the worthiness of content capsized. The result in popular music has been pristine sound polishing underbaked, though often overthought records.

Strive for transportations more than songs.

Allow space for the air surrounding the instruments.

Seek players that bring the songs to life.

One can be hounded more by sounds than sights—a family member's last breath, a lover climaxing, an ankle snapping and giving way.

I kept hearing one voice for the rest of my life, though I'd never seen the face.

These are possessions—memories that need not be recalled, but instead that we're unable to suppress.

VIII.

FAMILY RESEMBLANCE:

We're All Just Passing Through

50

Dangerously Similar Others:
False Friends

He threw a missing punch, just hanging there.
I knew I should run, but didn't.
And then he burst out laughing.
I'd called his bluff.
Like a catapult,
we were destined to become best friends.

There is nothing that one can hate quite as much as oneself, for there is no escape. We are quartered.

The common assumption is of neighbors being alike. But often they are even *more* inclined to resent one another due to sharing space, and the wars and disputes that can bring.

Like siblings mad-dogging each other over Thanksgiving dinner, the resemblance is too close for comfort. Border towns share each other's backwash.

The same dynamic drives my Rwandan mother-in-law to detest our daughter possessing a nappy-haired doll. She angrily insists that if we were fit parents, we would replace it posthaste with a white and "normal" one instead "like everybody else."

Ustad Saami surveys his own city
block, a world abuzz to itself.

Pakistan:
God Is Not a Terrorist

Hawks crowd the skies above Karachi as a blessing. They are fed scraps from animal sacrifices due to the prayers of the nonverbal being thought to reach God more powerfully.

Seventy-five-year-old Ustad Saami risks his life daily in Pakistan to keep alive his microtonal, pre-Islamic, multilingual (Farsi, Sanskrit, Hindi, the ancient and dead language of Vedic, gibberish, Arabic, and Urdu) music. He is the only vocal practitioner of *Surti* left in the world, which was handed down by his ancestors for over a thousand years, and when he passes, this music will most likely die with him as well. Extremists resent his work, as they do anything predating Muhammad.

In the land where Osama Bin Laden last hid, Master Ustad Naseeruddin Saami has spent his entire life mastering the nuances of every given note.

It has been said that India once had a region where all of the preeminent singers came from. And that place is Pakistan.

One of just nine countries to possess nuclear arms—and the only Islamic nation to do so—the Pakistani state is so feared that the governmental advisory was for its staff to not stay in hotels anywhere in the entire country—*any* hotel. About as daunting a travel warning as could be issued.

Driving in from the airport I noticed a man cleaning what I thought a musical instrument but then realized was a machine gun. Weaponry is another visual motif throughout the city. En route, we passed celebrity-soldier-sponsored billboards for house paint. Here, army officers carry a similar hollow cachet to reality stars in America.

"To sing is to listen." These are the words of the master. The translation of his own last name, Saami, even means "to hear."

For him, everything centers on one note. From that, all else grows and music is seen as a sixth sense for people to better communicate with each other.

Almost every musical system known starts with five notes and then enlarges as players add decoration through passing notes. With great precision, Saami utilizes forty-nine notes versus the West's mere seven. That means that for a single Western note, his customized Surti system contains the same number of intervals between each as is in our entire scale. The genesis of this Surti spectrum came from a mixed-race royal whose lifelong endeavor was to make peace with duality, and Ustad has cobbled his own vision together from multiple ancient sources. It is related to the predecessor to *Qawwali* music named *Khayál*, an Arabic word for "imagination" and in it the melody carries the meaning. The lyrics instead are almost incidental during these call-and-responses.

Ustad Saami believes that the rigid divisions of what are and are not notes has done "violence" to music and he is trying to restore "lost" pitches.

The much internationally hyped Qawwali music (due to Nusrat Fateh Ali Khan having been championed by a bona fide rock star in the 1980s) has mystic origins but is now used mostly for celebrations. Therefore, it is kept alive by what are essentially wedding singers and, as with all party music, has unavoidably been corrupted by its commercialization.

In contrast, Jazz's trajectory was the reverse. It started as commercial fare (barrelhouse-piano entertainment for brothels) that was melded into an art form by its inheritors. Jazz was the rare case where the shift from dancing to seated and close-listening music did not tame but resulted in greater abstraction.

Today, neophyte, urbane media moguls tell master Saami that he doesn't know how to sing, since his notes fail to align on their disinfected and dumbed-down grid. Engineers unable to see his notes on their Pro Tools program, assume that it's the artist and not the machine that is mistaken. But it is the uneven pitches that the master values. They are the most searching. Those with even numbers, too stable.

A compounding cultural force is that extremists strive to drive the music out of Islam, viewing it as having no place in a righteous society. So now instead of beckoning, the five calls to prayer are barked over intercoms around the clock, coarsely and off-pitch. The master's taking on female students is yet another sore point.

Harmonium, the instrument that is now so strongly associated with the region, was actually introduced by missionaries and banned from the radio until 1962. That was D-Day culturally for Pakistan. The instrument restricted music to off/on keys, excluding other possibilities.

Faced with fretted instruments in America, African abductees and their descendants simply picked up beer bottles and butter knives—along with any other household tool nearby—to slide across the neck, ignoring the dictated framework to instead float and hover over notes of their own design—literally transcending the sonic shackles that'd been imposed.

As we sat being interviewed by a local Karachi journalist in a hotel lobby, there was comedy to the endless loop of Christmas songs that impregnated every corner, and badly rendered MIDI versions, at that.

Pakistan was created by the largest mass migration in history as Muslims and non-Muslims swapped sides of the border. Most westward migrants ended up in the port city of Karachi with the promise that they would eventually be relocated and integrated throughout Pakistan. But that promise remains unfulfilled and these relative newcomers remain cordoned off throughout the city, with neighborhoods forming microregions that reflect wherever they migrated from in India before first alighting.

As he sings, Ustad shapes the notes with his hands like playing a Theremin. Most masters now hide their knowledge, possessively passing their skills down through family only. Subsequently, traditions have withered and died. Master Saami's mission is to share his knowledge freely with the world, so that the music can potentially continue on.

The emphasis on creating deadened rooms for recording has always struck me as a signifier of why so many records end up sounding lifeless. Though overdubbed recordings can layer sounds, they lack the sympathetic overtones that can only be created when elements physically coexist and resonate with one another in real time, beyond the control of anyone and anything but the elements at hand.

What antiseptic methods expunge are the sounds that are suggested, but not entirely there. Yet it is exactly whatever listeners imagine is happening that can be every bit as important as that which actually is. Saami's album was performed entirely live on his rooftop while accompanied by his sons who cradled and gently finger-plucked three-foot-high, hand-carved, family heirloom drones on either side of him.

With the musicians' tongues reddened and teeth devastated from chewing *paan*, we recorded all night long, taking only a brief break for a meal. In the morning, after the sun had come up, the younger players were understandably collapsed from exhaustion. The master, though, displayed markedly more energy than when we'd begun the night before. He urged the others to keep going, though unsuccessfully. His power proved too much for them to keep pace.

Not Nearly the Best, but Still Enough

I regularly mowed the lawn of an elderly neighbor who had a laugh that sounded more like hate. He'd sit shaded on his patio and watch me bake beneath the sun, then begrudgingly hand over whatever coins he could find in his pocket.

Eventually, I managed to save enough to buy my mother tickets to see Tom Jones, the only artist she'd ever expressed any interest in.

It was the height of his sex-god fame, and I found myself the only other male in a sold-out theater. For the duration of the concert, a procession of fans approached the stage. After waiting their turn, without missing a line Sir Jones would dutifully towel his neck and face with the handkerchief that each person came armed with. The women would then walk away squealing and often inhaling the scent.

My mother was too timid to advance forward. So I made my way slowly in the dark.

Ever the showman, he instantly spotted the gag—a nine-year-old fat kid had to be good for a laugh.

After having busted trashy, over-the-top poses for an hour, he gasped for breath and leaned down, showering me with sweat. The stage was strewn with bras, panties, and bouquets that had been hurled at his feet as offerings. He asked what it was that I wanted. He towered over me even more atop his platform heels.

"This is for my mom. But she's too shy."

It brought down the house. When I walked back to my seat, my mom hugged me harder than she ever had before, around the neck, as if it were for the last time.

It was at that moment that I knew that to elicit such happiness—no matter how fleeting—a singer's job must be among the most sacred to be found.

51

Fueled by Fear

An OB/GYN doctor told me that *every* woman she's attended during a delivery protests that they cannot go on with labor at the exact moment that it begins in earnest.

This is in much the same way that a majority of relationships splinter right as true intimacy—and the fright it brings—emerges. Through an overabundance of self-sabotage, legions leave the planet without ever knowing a deeper closeness to another.

Fear is at the heart of everything. But fear itself is not the issue. It is unacknowledged or denied fear that leads people to explode.

Anger is almost invariably a self-inflicted wound. It acts as a boomerang. We *make* ourselves mad, rather than actually being so to begin with. We think ourselves into it as a way to insulate from the underlying fear and sadness that angry states actually originate from.

The lie of catharsis is that a person can get something out of their system by intensifying it. But the existing frustration is only compounded unless one begins to deal with anger's root causes—the fear *of* fear that is being masked.

When we sing about love, we usually speak about pain, loss, and alienation. The majority of pop songs are indeed "love songs." But most are heartbreak songs.

The concentration on conflict and strife sets interpersonal dysfunction as the norm and keeps people arrested developmentally.

We talk about "feelings" without expressing them purely or accurately naming them. Most of us tumble into the trap of substituting thoughts or judgments for emotions—"I feel that is wrong" versus "I feel sad."

There is no greater lyrical hook than the word "you."

Statistically, the most frequently used word in English is the word "I," as is similarly the case in virtually every language that's been studied. That is why almost all advertising propaganda is based on flipping this around into "you" messages—making a mirror.

Imagine the free world's fate if Uncle Sam posters had proclaimed "We need some people" rather than "I want *you*," three simple one-syllable words accompanied by a pointed finger to reinforce the message and guarantee that *you* wouldn't miss the point. Ponder the trajectory pop music would've taken had the Beatles hit American shores with "I Want to Hold *Her* Hand" not "I Want to Hold Your Hand." ("Fuck her. Where is the part about *me*?")

No matter what the topic, people more often than not are talking about themselves.

Somaliland:
Stood Up by the Rock
Star . . . Again!

After their storage containers are emptied, semis race back across the border, jockeying to be first in line for a new load at the port. Locals call them "Al-Qaeda" trucks since they drive without brakes and multiple fatalities routinely result.

Along the way we passed biblical donkey road-kill and more stray camels than stray dogs. We tore through the lowest point in Africa— beneath the ocean where there is no ocean. Instead, it is one of the driest places on earth.

So few people travel on the main road north that the scant souvenir shops that do exist are kept shuttered. But unmarked, just a hundred yards east of a split-second swerve in the freeway, sits as breathtaking a canyon as can be found anywhere. Tourists here are counted in mere hundreds per year but should rightly be by the millions.

We set up there, on the cliff's edge utilizing the largest vintage reverb unit on the global market: the planet earth. As we recorded, a baby scorpion kept crawling atop my eight-track and arching its tail, seemingly supervising the input levels.

The search is not for what is explicitly "exotic" but anything *not* standardized. The musicians here had never heard of Tinariwen. They played their own self-styled "desert rock."

According to locals, musicians are "zombies" since they rise only after dark, too high from chewing *khat* all night before.

No one is exempt from the human race, no culture has a monopoly on sainthood or assholism.

Once in Blantyre, a local bigwig ran us around the city for a day, switching the rendezvous point and time, until finally revealing that he was not in the country the entire time. That later his fellow Malawians—the Mouse men as well as Zomba prison's inmates—achieved international attention that he could not rally for decades, seemed somehow cosmically just.

Our musician friend here claimed he didn't do the recording for the money, but as a favor to us. Nonetheless, we had to front him cash for his daily fix of plant leaves and cigarettes.

I was already leery. He'd come too heavily recommended. Few can justify that sort of buildup. As if on cue, he fell well short—refusing to continue after just three faltering and couch-laden takes.

It was the most picturesque recording experience I've ever had, but woefully among the least fruitful.

Nonetheless, he remained a legend in his own scene.

The hangers-on applauded as we returned.

52

Counting Your Curses

Decades down I can easily call up the hurt of my closest friend sharing how "lucky" he thought I was that my first love had been raped. He said it would give me something to write about. Instead of the consolation he'd intended, I felt even greater loss and estrangement.

Artists don't make great art because of the pain they are in. They produce in spite of it, as an attempt (though, often unsuccessful) to escape agony.

Trauma has a way of dispersing people. Dynamics are reset. Those closest often abandon and flee. Meanwhile, folks on the periphery sometimes step up to fill the relational void. Some do so for impure reasons—magnetized by the pain, attempting to warm themselves vicariously by drawing near, but still remaining not too close, keeping an easy out available.

It becomes almost a duty to take misfortune and transmute it into something constructive or even translucent. But that is a far cry from seeking out or self-inflicting such misery.

We can become energy converters, not obliged to remain passive recipients, but instead possessing potential as a destabilizing force—in positive or negative—by way of the net impact of our individual actions.

One of the mightiest things about creativity is that it can hijack anguish and reshape damaging experiences into something sublime. Loss gets easier with time, but never "easy."

Art can transform the world, making it less ugly. And that is the first purpose of creativity—the refusal to inertly accept the bad and sad that we've been dealt, to instead harness our grief for goodness.

My teenage goal was not fame, but connection. To give voice through mine to the collective pain my loved ones had endured, so that it would not have proven entirely without reason. The failure to make my words heard became a double devastation. I had not only let myself down, but also those I cherished most along with the concept of redemption itself.

Stories can act as burial grounds, bids to keep passion alive inside us for as long as possible, in tribute to those already fallen.

In the end, most pain is referential. It comes from somewhere else, more deeply rooted than the apparent source.

Three Scenes from the Same East Oakland Parking Lot

The Budweiser bottle shattered at my feet.

It was a greeting, tossed by some Hells Angels huddled thirty yards away. It was the same chapter that had infamously killed an African-American man in front of the stage at the Rolling Stones' Altamont festival atop the nearby hills, dividing the already suburban rednecks (such as myself) from the truly bedrock numbskulls of the agriculturally behemoth Central Valley of California.

They were issuing some sort of white trash baptism.

My father had reluctantly dropped me there at the curb of the arena, having steered our paneled station wagon through the tailgate parties.

I was a twelve-year-old, rolling solo to my first concert ever.

I ran the gauntlet of trough urinals inside where homophobia ran rampant. Cursed by a bashful bladder, after an extended and failed attempt I retreated, tiptoeing over adults passed out and unattended, face-down in their own puke.

Greater diversity could probably be found at a KKK rally.

With my head down, I climbed the cement stairs to the nosebleed seat awaiting me at the top row—the pot smoke hung so thick that it obscured what little could be seen of the stage from that distance.

Then Sammy Hagar hit the stage, dressed head to toe in red. He looked like a singing fire hydrant, setting the pre–Gangsta Rap record for spewing the word "fuck" the most times onstage. The music was vacuous, but the energy high as Monsieur Hagar milked his local-boy status for all it was worth.

"Even the motherfuckin' white boys think they're Prince now."

The line to enter the arena had come to a standstill. I knew they were talking about my stoner curls. I was the only white guy in sight. I tried ignoring them, but they persisted.

"Fucking faggot."

This seemed a particularly tone-deaf slur given Prince's blatant ambiguity about his sexuality, known to writhe around onstage in silk sheets and wearing nothing but bikini briefs, pumps, and eyeliner while simulating auto-erotic acts.

I was wearing a salvage-shop trench coat. Not because I thought it was cool, but because I worked as a janitor there—a clothing kennel, discarded items last chance of salvation before euthanasia. That coat was what I could afford.

"He looks like a fucking girl. Goldilocks! Shirley Temple."

I knew a shove to the back would come next. And by counting the voices, it was clear that I was outnumbered by at least four.

"I think he looks kind of cute," interjected their sole female companion, more in provocation than defense. And it was then that I knew it was on for sure.

All I'd wanted was to see Prince. He'd just released *Sign o' the Times*, and the opening verse featured some of the most literate lyrics ever to crack the Top Ten. Somehow I'd been able to find a single ticket to a long-sold-out show.

I played dead. As hard as he pushed me, I refused to turn around until finally the energy folded back on him. His girlfriend intervened and started slapping *him*.

Then the line moved, at last.

Music had brought us together but failed to heal. Within the hour we'd be singing along to the same songs. For us they held different meanings.

The most unforgettable Springsteen show I ever saw I actually couldn't see and only heard. From the parking lot, we stood stranded, unable to score tickets out front. The songs lacerated as they rose up over the lip of the bleachers and bounced against the freeway, then ping-ponged around the parking lot. Occasionally an audience roar would rise. Undoubtedly, some exaggerated pose had been struck.

But what we were left with was washes of melody, the low-end remaining trapped inside, ground to a mushy thud entwined with the crackle of out-of-phase hi-hat hits and barre chords dried by the autumn air.

As a populist singer, "the Boss" never sounded better than to the ragtag few who weren't privileged enough to gain entrance—ones who knew the words to every song but couldn't take part in the staged singalong. We were gathered outside with the ticket scalpers from the neighborhood who couldn't give two shits about what artist they'd just conned the fans of. Instead, they counted their stacks of twenties and headed home over the pedestrian bridge to the BART trains.

One seller had taunted me, "Why do all you people want to see this dude, anyway? There's no way anybody can get down to this shit." And he was spot-on about its colossality, the vacuum of polyrhythm.

Disingenuousness set in when Springsteen hushed the crowd for a solo acoustic version of Woody Guthrie's "This Land Is Your Land" and reached the lines:

> There was a big high wall there
> that tried to stop me.
> Sign was painted.
> It said, "No trespassing."
> But on the back side
> It didn't say nothing.

On the streets of West Oakland, Bea belts with a
vulnerability rarely found anywhere.

The Land of Aplenty:
A City in the Key of D♭

I have been to Kibera, arguably the world's largest slum, a place where human shit runs in the streets.

But I've never seen poverty more severe than here.

I'd come home. To my birthplace: Oakland.

Homeless encampments cling beneath freeway overpasses like albatross, enlarging daily, fed in reverse by the excesses of tech-enabled hypercapitalism—our home-grown, capitalistic terrorism.

Crack dealers stand sentry over most encampments with chained pit bulls at the ready. The tent clusters are contoured with baby-carriage carnage and a super mashup of stolen shopping carts.

Most everywhere people now tend towards rapping rather than crooning if asked to communicate musically—their words born from slang and boasts. An untold aspect of poverty is that it suffocates the basic drive to express oneself—let alone the instruments to do so or the willingness of listeners to be attentive. Great truths have been muttered in response to voices inside the stricken's head—shouted into the wind, ignored.

Sadly, the transient community's talent pool is almost limitless. And growing by the day.

One woman, Bea, sleeps on a couch sunken under the freeway. She emerged from her sole blanket cover and within seconds launched into a free-association song about the loss of hope that followed her mother's passing. It was a gut-wrenching but seemingly effortless declaration of grief, waged through toothless gums. She went straight from sleep to baring her soul, with zero pretense.

The self-identified musicians were not as forthcoming.

One refused to record, stating he was going on tour to Paris. We found him days later, crashed out on a park bench instead.

Another elderly man claimed that his debut album was forthcoming and that a cover had been shot by a "real" photographer. Wallowing in this reverie, he then escalated abruptly, leaping to his feet, spitting through his beard, and attempting to square off with me, an eight-inch sheathed blade banging against his hip like a seismograph of his instability. He'd not counted on this scenario resembling too closely ones I'd played out far too many times on locked psychiatric wards. Recognizing that his posturing had not produced the desired effect, he deflated, and we parted friends.

Working in that very county's psychiatric emergency room for over a decade, the staff were left to untangle whether an individual's mental health condition had led to homelessness or homelessness itself had caused the affliction. We were straddled by laws that made violence the determining factor whether someone would receive treatment. The "dangerous" were assisted, the peaceful left to fend for themselves or perish.

On an offramp corner, a young lady stood for days, soiled and with unintentional dreadlocks. She wore sole-less Disney princess shoes, sizes too small, and clutched a water bottle laced with miscellaneous microchip parts. Her eyes were at constant drift for dangers she'd recognized too late. She was as vulnerable as someone left for dead on a sidewalk. And she had been. The police passed but could not be waved down.

As a systemic symbol, the recurrent maimed wheelchairs in which many arrived at our hospital doors were as apt as any—disabled people living on the streets with disabled devices. Or the cases of scabies that were left untreated for so long that layers of clothing had furrowed and grafted onto the skin, laced deep down into the dermis like third-degree burns to the point that reconstructive surgery was required.

Now, many cash-strapped social-service programs have been gobbled up by tech companies, with practitioners forced to spend more time on computers than with clients. The giant corporations are invested to ingest data on homelessness—churning destitution into data—profiting from poverty rather than alleviating it.

At Zomba Prison in Malawi, a giant of a guard once blocked my exit and demanded, "Are there any poor people in America?"

When I replied that there were, he poked me hard in the rib with his knuckle and persisted, "No! I mean *really* poor people. People with no shoes."

I pondered this for a moment and then told him that such people actually did exist in the USA, that usually they were homeless.

That word stopped him. Even in the world's number-one poorest nation, such a concept did not exist. No matter how tiny a clay-and-thatch hut, almost no one was ever turned away from it without shelter.

He shook his head in pity, unable to match or top it. America had prevailed again.

This inhumanity occurs not due to lack of wealth but will.

Homelessness is a war crime that we're all complicit in, to varying degrees.

The more that any single individual is overexalted and indulged, the less that human life as a whole must be cheapened to compensate.

The day that a person first stepped over another passed out on a sidewalk was as monumental a cultural moment as Neil Armstrong walking on the moon.

The resulting slaughter fills our streets.

Look Away from the Flash

As a child visiting my mother's tiny-towned birthplace in eastern Kansas, fireflies would ignite the sky, and we'd trap them in jars to use as flickering flashlight to navigate the cornfields. I'd lie awake, transfixed by the street lamp outside. The bar patrons next door were shrouded behind a fence, and their rumblings animated the insects that swarmed, yellowing the rays. It was hard to distinguish the more intelligent life form.

Back home, my parents would take us in our station wagon to drive-in double features. The charge was by the carload on "Family Night." To save even more money, my mom would skillet-fry popcorn at home and then portion it into paper lunch sacks, the butter and salt soaking through and dripping onto the car interior.

With seats folded flat, we'd lie back and when a movie turned slow, rotate and watch the opposing screen mismatched to the sound of our own—Clint Eastwood dubbed by Disney (*Dirty Harry* meets *Herbie Rides Again*). I discovered that what occurred incidentally was often far more interesting than the intentional.

In much the same way, on planes I often prefer to watch images with no sound and in fragments from other people's monitors, leaving the content more enigmatic. The juxtaposition of asynchronous vignettes can elevate even a going-through-the-motions Hollywood romcom to something more.

As a genre, the allure of silent film has returned today via the ever-popular CCTV security footage follies.

In my long-gone era, there was an XXX-rated drive-in set among the orchards and farms lining Sacramento to San Francisco, a stretch that has since filled almost completely as one exit after another's strip mall and tract-home developments duplicated.

The screen there was strategically angled away from the highway to tease those passing. It was not possible to make out any lone detail, except the furthest fuzzy edge where the light spilled over and around. What was depicted in those flickering projections was no doubt far less erotic than what it fired inside our skulls.

We were shielded from nipples and vaginas, but not from guns.

Thousands of drawn guns.

53

Interlaced

And so I stood. One of two American white guys about to throw down in a foreign country, on a crowded train. All over a suitcase's position, and with my daughter in tow.

I didn't feel afraid, just ashamed.

It seemed in that one meat-headed, micromoment the entirety of post-WWII imperialism was playing out another encore.

The crowd of strangers regarded us patronizingly—as if we were befitting of mercy, that our idiocy made our citizenship self-evident.

Nearing the station, I wondered what his favorite song was, if it sounded like anything other than grinding gears and hate. This young man who was calling me "dick" for the first time since junior high school, a stranger professing that I was "nothing."

I flashbacked on the more than decade of verbal abuse I'd withstood daily working in psychiatric emergency. And I waited for what felt like generations.

I waited until the willingness to listen prevailed again.

He shook my hand before walking away.

I am not the hero in this tale. I am the punchline. I failed him, myself, everyone. But at least I was able to recover, in part, before it was too late. And for that modest mark, I give thanks.

54

Meek Inheritance

My wife looked exactly like her father. An Italian face with darker skin and curls. But locals could never see past the color.

And the same is now true with my daughter, who is even a lighter shade and looks more my twin than my offspring. To my wife, people insist, "She's *all* you."

In a region where cops with shaved eyebrows do not register a single raised brow, the Labor and Delivery ward janitor was so unable to recognize any resemblance between myself and my daughter that she had the audacity to suggest that my wife had cuckolded me, a familiarity never dared towards anyone that wasn't other—particularly amid Italy's highly formalized social code.

"How come you speak such good Italian?" my wife is quizzed almost daily, often by white foreigners. Meanwhile, fellow citizens routinely respond with English to her perfect Italian, making clear that she doesn't belong.

Contrastingly, nearly everywhere we go in our travels, she is claimed: "You could be one of us"—a different, slightly more benign prejudice.

I hope that my daughter will never have to share a passage like this. Even more, my wish is that someday she would find such sentiments dated if she ever read them.

But sadly these words could've been written at almost any time throughout human history. We are perpetually straddled by the myth that we are modern, that we exist beyond now.

Ignorance springs forth, perennial. And without vigilance, overtakes it.

55

The Straw That *Saves* the Camel's Back

Depression is engraved in the faces of many Italians—palpable pathos, depths of despair as ground zero. But the suicide rate remains one of the world's lowest, less than a quarter that of the United States.

Why?

A plate of hand-cut pasta stands before the abyss. It is not that good food can act as a clinical cure, but as a stave.

Anyone mistaking that I am being crass, I am not. Three of the people I loved most in this world took their own life. Yet this is as good an explanation as any for the statistical discrepancy.

A fingered chord radiating up your arm—music not just heard, but felt, is a counterbalance, a restoration.

With the spoon she used as a mallet, my toddler would stop and try to eat the sound from concave drums—further proof that insight need not correspond to chronological age.

The music was feeding her.

56

CONCLUSION
Strong Silent Types:
Walk Quietly and
Carry a Big Think

As postindustrialized citizens, we have a responsibility to try to take back and reclaim the noise that mechanization has subjected us to and, instead, make it our own. Noise is customarily so looked down upon that most people use the word to describe any music that they disapprove of.

Ironically, instruments themselves were the first small step towards materialism in music, thereby, divorcing ourselves in part from it.

Owning an instrument does not make someone a musician. Some of the most musical people I've ever met have never touched one. But they *live* musically—every moment, every day.

Virtuosity is not necessarily a virtue. Many fastidiously trained professionals have forgotten how to fuck and/or never really learned to dance.

Children being scolded that they are not musical—that they should shut up and *not* sing—constitutes an all-too-common act of abuse.

Diversity proves good in genetics, beneficial with nutrition. So the question follows: do we really need to hear the same song—no matter how fine—hundreds of times in a lifetime? Could not our ears and neurons be put to better use challenged by the new?

Instruments are just tools and need be no more intimidating than a pen or plunger. They are merely means to an end, and their over-reverence is just another form of consumerism—one that fervent people fall into when buying vintage guitars that cost more than cars.

Big bands were wiped out by guitar amps that could match their muscle with only a trio or quartet. Charlie Christian had turned up as he simply wanted his guitar heard—lifted from background to soloist—but before long, guitar was almost all that was heard. Later, party DJs rolled along to mop up what remnants of collaboration were left, underselling even more the downsized ensemble labor forces.

Among our most notable features is how noisy we are, regardless of its unintentionality. While other species thrive on stealth, humans luxuriate atop the food chain—almost incapable of walking on cat's paws.

With much study, outsiders could make sense of the patterns of our speech, but not our music since the notes fail to carry precise meaning. That's part of their power—the veil.

Or perhaps instead pop music would translate to something like, "I am stuck and empty." More optimistically, music as its hardiest maybe already is communicating with a higher intelligence (at least within ourselves) or "the beyond."

Our entire body acts as an ear. And the earth is a drum. One which has been played haphazardly since the dawn of the Industrial Age.

Evil screams. But peace permeates. For it is everywhere. The good must not be lost amid horror. We best turn our attention instead towards what is most prevalent, not most evident.

Listen to the reluctant.

Ignore the demanding.

Seek out those forgotten and overlooked.

Help bring something beautiful into the world (... and try not to make too much of a mess along the way).

57

EPILOGUE Mother Tongues: you, with highlights in your hair that could scare away the sun

Long before my mother's hopes folded back in on her, a surgeon cut out most of her intestine. She was twenty-six years old, and it changed the course of her life.

This mishap occurred due to her regular doctor being away on vacation—a golf holiday, as if the cliché didn't exacerbate the impact. The MD subbing for him was a butcher, a hack.

My mother's life was never the same. Therefore, neither was mine. And I was not yet even born.

Something gave way, deep. She walled off that part of herself. And said goodbye.

She spent the reminder of her life pouring herself between the fissures in her life.

It led me to a healthy distrust of experts.

I also hold great respect for many of them but believe that far too many of us die by blind faith—that always getting a second opinion is not a suggestion, but a rule. Further, any authority that attempts to dissuade us from doing so, should be dismissed without pause.

In the psychiatric emergency room where I worked in Oakland, three psychiatrists were convicted of separate felonies in an eighteen-month period. That demystified authority even more—another usurping of the intellect's mistaken primacy over emotional maturity and integrated intelligence.

Intellect without insight can easily be weaponized. That is likely why Martin Luther King Jr. included in his inner circle many musicians rather than politicians, finding that they offered perspectives mere academics often could not.

It is regret that prevents the ability to inch forward and heal. If one is bound by the torture of knowing there were alternate outcomes—that there was something else that could've been done to thwart tragedy— the trauma becomes almost impassable.

And that's what happened with my mother.

I grew up in the wake of my parents gutted dreams, my mother's former self trailing her around the house like a carcass, a load that doubled her and was far more than she could bear.

A farm girl, the energy of city life infected and eventually rewired her entire nervous system.

One day I came home from grade school to her holding my father's pistol for fear that on our little suburban street, there were intruders outside. More than once, squad cars jammed our driveway.

When I would open the door to the back room where she'd retreat, there was the sensation of breaking something sealed. There was a stillness devoid of residual reverberance, as if she had not moved— even minutely—for hours.

She broke almost everything she touched. Coffee mugs, door locks, shirt-sleeve buttons—even little objects suffered her existential clumsiness. She'd never learned to care for things, as she herself had not been cared for properly.

She failed at almost everything, even suicide. But she never wavered towards me.

She was unable to raise her voice except to scream. Then, all of that yielding would come unhinged, words unfurled like shards of glass— they expressed hurt rather than being designed to hurt.

She was not a music fan, couldn't even match artists to songs. The only one that she knew by heart was "Danny Boy." She could recite the first few lines and then had to hum her way through the rest, before trailing off entirely. It was the lone tune her dad, a reticent man, had ever sung. Few could sing a song of devotion to one's child more poignantly than a person who'd been abandoned before age ten by his own father.

If karma existed, my mother would have lived to be a hundred-and-three. But, alas . . .

We were in the hills of Rwanda as you passed. Almost as far astray as could be, but as good a second place as any, if there could be one at all: Adrien was singing when you left this world.

I know now that if only I could lift my head up far enough, I could still see you.

58

REQUIEM

The day that citizens of Indonesia or Burkina Faso scour America in search of "authentic music"—shoving iPhones into the locals' faces, snapping pictures without permission, and rightly pondering what on earth ever happened to the USA's deep well of vibrant sound—would be a fair and just one indeed. If ever white church choirs were forced into supporting-roles only—even in deference to clearly lesser singers—then grouped in half-lit combos and instructed to sway and smile *behind* African-American soloists. That would be all the richer.

Instruments derive from and are a *potential* link back to the spiritual world. In order to connect more fully with all music—that outside of the prescribed elements—we must overcome and deliberately break free from the prison and repetitive structures of Western sounds that constrict listening and keep people feeling safe and even infantilized instead of challenged.

So, whenever the chance arises, hum some made-up ditty to your child (or yourself) rather than subjecting them to "Smoke on the Water" or "I Will Always Love You" for the umpteenth time. Ad-lib your own ragtag bedtime tale rather than hitting play on *Toy Story* ad nauseam.

And if you are ever even fortunate enough to experience a double amputee throat-singing in the Oriya language or to hear a lesbian, Filipino-Irish, hardcore punk Cumbia trio rock out versus listening yet one more time to _____ (insert name of your choice here)

… well, I think we all know what the right thing to do is.

AFTERWORD

Overview
of Key Points

1. Written music was the first form of recording.
   a) It began a division between musical and nonmusical people, literate and illiterate.

2. Recording is inherently a conservative action. Often what it preserves might have otherwise been a transient moment or impulse, not necessarily a reflection of any tradition.

3. The superstar system promotes the concept of heroic authorship, according to which one individual is believed to be gifted beyond the reach of mere mortals.
   a) Genius is generally only afforded to individuals from the ruling class. Instead underlings' artistic efforts are viewed as arising from their "people" and history, from the past, not the present or future, or themselves.

4. When corporations and governments ran out of physical space to conquer, they began instead colonizing time (e.g., future generations' environmental quality of life) and attention itself. The infinity promised by digital technology denies the reality that *we* are not infinite. These are the hidden costs of the internet, the shell game of making things incarnate. Limits persist and every "free" thing comes with a price—the investment of our limited time, energy, and consciousness.
   a) Self-cannibalizing, Artificial Intelligence-generated content curation builds algorithmic prisons.

Some Possible Solutions

1. Volunteerism as a counter-demonstration that experiences can have value without being measured by money.

    2. Unconditional giving.

    3. Anonymous authorship.

    4. Practicing doubt.

    5. Policing and foregrounding subtext.

6. Refusing to support disposable music (even if done so ironically).
    a) Instead, devote energies to what ignites our sincere passion. There is too much unloved, quality music lost to waste our affections on shite.

For the Record(s): Unfair Trade

I don't own a house.

Or a car.

Halfway to a hundred and about the only things I have to my name are a few microphones and far too many boxes of books.

And I stand to inherit almost nothing.

Marilena and I earn no profits from these projects. But nonetheless we always ensure that the artists are paid something out of our own pocket, however modest it may be.

These are money-losing acts of love.

That said, I would love to make a million one day, to at least provide some stability for my family. But that is not the driving goal, nor does it seem in any way forthcoming.

I have already been evicted once in my life. Not for being anything less than a model tenant, but simply due to the greed of an affluent landlord willing to throw me out of my hometown for a few extra bucks.

I've reached a stage where years are no longer counted. Time is tracked by deaths instead. But I have yet to relinquish faith in the power of song.

Far from a saint, I am flawed. I am acutely aware, that no one has benefited more from these experiences than me, far in excess of any currency.

I stand in the debt of strangers.

The author recording on the Horn of Africa, using
his favorite vintage reverb unit: the planet earth.

ABOUT THE AUTHOR

Ian Brennan is a Grammy-winning music producer who has also produced three Grammy-nominated albums. He is also the author of five books and has worked with the likes of filmmaker John Waters, Fugazi, Merle Haggard, Tinariwen, and Green Day, among others. His work with international artists such as the Zomba Prison Project, Tanzania Albinism Collective, and Khmer Rouge Survivors, has been featured on the front page of the *New York Times* and on an Emmy-winning segment for the television program *60 Minutes* with Anderson Cooper reporting.

He also has taught violence prevention and conflict resolution around the world since 1993 for such prestigious organizations as the University of London, the New School, Berklee College of Music, the Smithsonian, Bellevue Hospital (NYC), the Betty Ford Clinic, UC Berkeley, and the National Accademia of Science (Rome).

Of his previous book, *How Music Dies (or Lives): Field Recording and the Battle for Democracy in the Arts, Hi-Fi Choice* magazine stated, "It's not often that you read a book that changes the way you listen to music ... if you only read one book about music this year, I strongly recommend that you make it this one," while *R2 (Rock 'n' Reel)* magazine raved, "Beg, borrow, or buy a copy of this important book now." *Songlines* magazine claimed it is "a thought-provoking read that challenges our preconceptions on almost every page."

ABOUT PM PRESS

PM Press was founded at the end of 2007 by a small
collection of folks with decades of publishing, media, and
organizing experience. PM Press co-conspirators have
published and distributed hundreds of books, pamphlets,
CDs, and DVDs. Members of PM have founded enduring
book fairs, spearheaded victorious tenant organizing campaigns, and worked
closely with bookstores, academic conferences, and even rock bands to deliver
political and challenging ideas to all walks of life. We're old enough to know what
we're doing and young enough to know what's at stake.

We seek to create radical and stimulating fiction and nonfiction books, pamphlets,
T-shirts, visual and audio materials to entertain, educate, and inspire you. We
aim to distribute these through every available channel with every available
technology—whether that means you are seeing anarchist classics at our bookfair
stalls, reading our latest vegan cookbook at the café, downloading geeky fiction
e-books, or digging new music and timely videos from our website.

PM Press is always on the lookout for talented and skilled volunteers, artists,
activists, and writers to work with. If you have a great idea for a project or can
contribute in some way, please get in touch.

PM Press
PO Box 23912
Oakland, CA 94623
www.pmpress.org

PM Press in Europe
europe@pmpress.org
www.pmpress.org.uk

FRIENDS OF PM PRESS

These are indisputably momentous times—the financial system is melting down globally and the Empire is stumbling. Now more than ever there is a vital need for radical ideas.

In the years since its founding—and on a mere shoestring—PM Press has risen to the formidable challenge of publishing and distributing knowledge and entertainment for the struggles ahead. With over 300 releases to date, we have published an impressive and stimulating array of literature, art, music, politics, and culture. Using every available medium, we've succeeded in connecting those hungry for ideas and information to those putting them into practice.

Friends of PM allows you to directly help impact, amplify, and revitalize the discourse and actions of radical writers, filmmakers, and artists. It provides us with a stable foundation from which we can build upon our early successes and provides a much-needed subsidy for the materials that can't necessarily pay their own way. You can help make that happen—and receive every new title automatically delivered to your door once a month—by joining as a Friend of PM Press. And, we'll throw in a free T-shirt when you sign up.

Here are your options:

- **$30 a month** Get all books and pamphlets plus 50% discount on all webstore purchases

- **$40 a month** Get all PM Press releases (including CDs and DVDs) plus 50% discount on all webstore purchases

- **$100 a month** Superstar—Everything plus PM merchandise, free downloads, and 50% discount on all webstore purchases

For those who can't afford $30 or more a month, we have **Sustainer Rates** at $15, $10 and $5. Sustainers get a free PM Press T-shirt and a 50% discount on all purchases from our website.

Your Visa or Mastercard will be billed once a month, until you tell us to stop. Or until our efforts succeed in bringing the revolution around. Or the financial meltdown of Capital makes plastic redundant. Whichever comes first.

The Explosion of Deferred Dreams: Musical Renaissance and Social Revolution in San Francisco, 1965–1975

Mat Callahan

ISBN: 978-1-62963-231-5
$22.95   352 pages

As the fiftieth anniversary of the Summer of Love floods the media with debates and celebrations of music, political movements, "flower power," "acid rock," and "hippies," *The Explosion of Deferred Dreams* offers a critical re-examination of the interwoven political and musical happenings in San Francisco in the Sixties. Author, musician, and native San Franciscan Mat Callahan explores the dynamic links between the Black Panthers and Sly and the Family Stone, the United Farm Workers and Santana, the Indian Occupation of Alcatraz and the San Francisco Mime Troupe, and the New Left and the counterculture.

Callahan's meticulous, impassioned arguments both expose and reframe the political and social context for the San Francisco Sound and the vibrant subcultural uprisings with which it is associated. Using dozens of original interviews, primary sources, and personal experiences, the author shows how the intense interplay of artistic and political movements put San Francisco, briefly, in the forefront of a worldwide revolutionary upsurge.

A must-read for any musician, historian, or person who "was there" (or longed to have been), *The Explosion of Deferred Dreams* is substantive and provocative, inviting us to reinvigorate our historical sense-making of an era that assumes a mythic role in the contemporary American zeitgeist.

"*Mat Callahan was a red diaper baby lucky to be attending a San Francisco high school during the 'Summer of Love.' He takes a studied approach, but with the eye of a revolutionary, describing the sociopolitical landscape that led to the explosion of popular music (rock, jazz, folk, R&B) coupled with the birth of several diverse radical movements during the golden 1965–1975 age of the Bay Area. Callahan comes at it from every angle imaginable (black power, anti-Vietnam War, the media, the New Left, feminism, sexual revolution—with the voice of authority backed up by interviews with those who lived it.*"
—Pat Thomas, author of *Listen, Whitey! The Sights and Sounds of Black Power 1965–1975*

"*All too often, people talk about the '60s without mentioning our music and the fun we had trying to smash the state and create a culture based upon love. Mat Callahan's book is a necessary corrective.*"
—George Katsiaficas, author of *The Imagination of the New Left: A Global Analysis of 1968*

One Chord Wonders: Power and Meaning in Punk Rock

Dave Laing
with a Foreword by TV Smith

ISBN: 978-1-62963-033-5
$17.95   224 pages

Originally published in 1985, *One Chord Wonders* was
the first full-length study of the glory years of British
punk rock. The book argues that one of punk's most
significant political achievements was to expose the
operations of power in the British entertainment industries as they were thrown
into confusion by the sound and the fury of musicians and fans.

Through a detailed examination of the conditions under which punk emerged
and then declined, Dave Laing develops a view of the music as both complex
and contradictory. Special attention is paid to the relationship between punk and
the music industry of the late 1970s, in particular the political economy of the
independent record companies through which much of punk was distributed. The
rise of punk is also linked to the febrile political atmosphere of Britain in the mid-
1970s.

Using examples from a wide range of bands, individual chapters use the
techniques of semiology to consider the radical approach to naming in punk (from
Johnny Rotten to Poly Styrene), the instrumental and vocal sound of the music, and
its visual images. Another section analyses the influence of British punk in Europe
prior to the music's division into "real punk" and "post-punk" genres.

The concluding chapter critically examines various theoretical explanations of the
punk phenomenon, including the class origins of its protagonists and the influential
view that punk represented the latest in a line of British youth "subcultures." There
is also a chronology of the punk era, plus discographies and a bibliography.

"A clear, unprejudiced account of a difficult subject."
—Jon Savage, author of *England's Dreaming*